ATARI ST
ST BASIC to C

Olaf Hartwig

A Data Becker Book from

Second Printing, May 1988
Printed in U.S.A.
Copyright © 1986

Copyright © 1986

Data Becker GmbH
Merowingerstr.30
4000 Dusseldorf, West Germany
Abacus Software, Inc.
P.O. Box 7219
Grand Rapids, MI 49510

This book is copyrighted. No part of this book may be reproduced, stored in a retrieval system, or transmitted in any form or by any means, electronic, mechanical, photocopying, recording or otherwise without the prior written permission of Abacus Software or Data Becker, GmbH.

Every effort has been made to insure complete and accurate information concerning the material presented in this book. However Abacus Software can neither guarantee nor be held legally responsible for any mistakes in printing or faulty instructions contained in this book. The authors will always appreciate receiving notice of subsequent mistakes.

ATARI, 520ST, ST, TOS, ST BASIC and ST LOGO are trademarks or registered trademarks of Atari Corp.

GEM, GEM Draw and GEM Write are trademarks or registered trademarks of Digital Research Inc.

IBM is a registered trademark of International Business Machines.

ISBN   0-916439-58-5

Table of Contents

Chapter 1 Development, applications, and the C language   1

Chapter 2 First steps for (former) BASIC programmers   7

2.1	Learn the elementary structures of C in one day	9
2.2	Functions and text output to the screen	10
2.3	Program format	12
2.4	Numerical screen output	13
2.4.1	Variable declarations	14
2.4.2	Initializing variables	15
2.4.3	The format instructions	15
2.5	Loops and comments	17
2.5.1	The `for` loop	17
2.5.2	The `while` loop	20
2.5.3	Comments in C	22
2.6	Data input	23
2.6.1	The `getchar()` function	23
2.6.2	The Alcyon C `getchar()`	25
2.6.3	The `scanf` function	26
2.6.4	The Alcyon C `scanf()`	27
2.6.5	Further use of variables in programs	27
2.7	Arithmetic in C	28
2.7.1	Similarities to BASIC	28
2.7.2	Differences from BASIC	29
2.7.3	The increment and decrement operators	31
2.8	More control structures in C	32
2.8.1	The `if` statement	32
2.8.2	The `if-else` statement	33
2.9	Data types in C	35
2.9.1	Variables	35
2.9.2	Constants	35
2.9.3	Arrays	36

Chapter 3 The basic elements of C   39

3.1	Program structure	41
3.2	Comments	42
3.3	Screen output	42
3.4	Variables and constants	43
3.5	Loops	44
3.6	Data input	44
3.7	Arithmetic in C	45
3.8	The if-else control structure	45

Chapter 4 Screen Input/Output Operations   47

4.1	Outputting text on the screen	49
4.2	Printing numerical values	50
4.3	Format instructions	52
4.3.1	Conversion elements	52
4.3.1.1	Numerical output	52
4.3.1.2	Character output	53
4.3.2	Format specifiers	53
4.3.3	Examples of numeric output	54
4.3.4	Text formatting	56
4.3.5	More uses for conversions and formats	56
4.4	Printing string variables on the screen	58
4.4.1	Printing a single character	60
4.4.2	More screen output	61
4.4.3	Additional output possibilities	62
4.5	Data input functions	65
4.5.1	The `getchar()` function	66
4.5.2	Input with `gets()`	67
4.5.3	The `scanf` input function	68
4.5.3.1	`scanf` for character and string input	69
4.5.3.2	Arrays in place of pointers	70
4.5.3.3	Entering numbers via `scanf`	71
4.5.3.4	Entering multiple data	72
4.5.4	The `GET$/INKEY$` function in C	73
4.5.5	Implementing `putchar()`, `getchar()` and `getch()` on Alcyon C for the Atari ST	74

Chapter 5 Variable Types in C   77

    5.1   Variable names   79
    5.2   Constants   81
    5.3   Data types   83
    5.4   Converting data types   84
    5.4.1   Character/integer conversion   84
    5.4.2   Converting between numeric types   87
    5.5   Variable declarations   88
    5.6   Global/local variables   90
    5.7   Arrays   91
    5.7.1   Multi-dimensional arrays   94
    5.7.2   Strings   94

Chapter 6 C Pointers   97

    6.1   Pointer fundamentals   99
    6.2   Using pointers   102
    6.3   Pointers and arrays   102
    6.4   Numeric arrays   103
    6.5   Strings and arrays   106

Chapter 7 Arithmetic Operators and Expressions   109

    7.1   What are operators?   111
    7.2   Value assignments   112
    7.3   The `modulo` operator   114
    7.4   The increment and decrement operators   115
    7.5   Comparison operators   117
    7.6   Logical combinations   119
    7.7   The negation operator   120
    7.8   Multiple assignments   122
    7.9   The bit operators   123

Chapter 8 Control Structures in C   125

    8.1   Control structures in BASIC   127
    8.2   The `if` statement   128
    8.2.1   The `exit()` statement   132

8.2.2	The `if-else` test	133
8.2.3	Combining `if-else` statements	134
8.2.4	`else-if` chains	135
8.3	`for` loops	136
8.3.1	Review and summary	137
8.3.2	Infinite loops	138
8.3.3	The comma operator	140
8.3.4	Nested `for` loops	141
8.4	`while` loops	145
8.4.1	Combinations of `for` and `while` loops	147
8.4.2	Nested `while` loops	148
8.4.3	The `do-while` loop	149
8.5	`break` for leaving loops	150
8.6	The `continue` statement	152
8.7	The `goto` jump	154
8.7.1	The `goto` syntax	154
8.7.2	Avoiding `goto`s	156
8.7.3	Applications for `goto`	156
8.8	Conditional execution with `switch`	157
8.8.1	Example	157
8.8.2	The `switch` syntax	158

Chapter 9 Common Mistakes of BASIC Programmers 163

9.1	Error # 1	165
9.2	Error # 2	166
9.3	Error # 3	167
9.4	Error # 4	168
9.5	Error # 5	168
9.6	Error # 6	169
9.7	Error # 7	170
9.8	Error # 8	171
9.9	Error # 9	172
9.10	Error #10	172
9.11	Error #11	173
9.12	Error #12	174
9.13	Error #13	174
9.14	Error #14	175

9.15	Error #15	176
9.16	Error #16	176
9.17	Error #17	177
9.18	Error #18	178
9.19	Error #19	179

Chapter 10 C Functions 181

10.1	Fundamentals of functions	184
10.1.1	Calling functions	184
10.1.2	Functions without parameters	185
10.1.3	Functions calling each other	188
10.2	Passing parameters to functions	190
10.2.1	Returning integer data	192
10.2.2	Returning other numerical data types	194
10.2.3	Pointers, functions and simultaneous parameter passing	195
10.3	The `DEF FN` command	197

Chapter 11 Structures 201

11.1	Declaring structures	203
11.2	Use of structure variables	204
11.3	Arrays and structures	206

Chapter 12 An overview of C 209

12.1	Keywords in C	211
12.2	C language statements	213
12.2.1	The `break` statement	213
12.2.2	The `case` statement	213
12.2.3	The `continue` statement	214
12.2.4	The `#define` statement	214
12.2.5	The `default` statement	215
12.2.6	The `do` statement	215
12.2.7	The `else` statement	216
12.2.8	The `else if` statement	216
12.2.9	The `for` statement	216

12.2.10	The goto statement	217
12.2.11	The if statement	217
12.2.12	The null statement	217
12.2.13	The return statement	218
12.2.14	The struct statement	218
12.2.15	The switch statement	219
12.2.16	The while statement	220
12.3	Variable types in C	221
12.3.1	Integer variables	221
12.3.2	Floating-point variables	221
12.4	Operators in C	222

Appendix A   225

Appendix B   227

Index   229

Chapter 1

Introduction to the C language

Development, applications, and the C language

C is a universal high-level programming language. This relatively new language was developed in the early 70's by Dennis Ritchie at Bell Laboratories (AT&T).

Many software designers consider C to be the programming language of the future. The most important reason for this is its compact syntax, which allows very concise expressions and programming structures close to the machine level.

C is also considered an "easy assembler" because compiling a C program generates pure machine code. Many C language programmers once programmed in machine language.

C is relatively close to the machine language level. This means that C works with the same objects (i.e. characters, numbers, and memory addresses) as the microprocessor. This feature is largely responsible for C's popularity for developing professional software. Nearly all high-performance software packages, such as the Lotus 1-2-3 spreadsheet and Ashton-Tate's dBASE III database manager, are written in C.

What interests us is that many programs for the Atari ST and the GEM operating system are written in C.

C is a very compact language. It has about the same number of language elements as BASIC. Therefore it should not be too difficult to learn the C language and syntax quickly.

The great strength of C lies in the number and variety of functions stored in *libraries*. The user can use these functions for all of his applications. With easy access to libraries, it is not necessary for the programmer to "reprogram" these functions over and over again. Features such as drop-down menus or dialog boxes are easily performed using the library functions of GEM. GEM is actually a collection of C library functions.

Because C is so much closer to the machine level than COBOL, Pascal, or BASIC, many programmers have difficulty switching over to C.

This applies especially to BASIC programmers. The change from BASIC to C is not easy if you have extensive BASIC experience. One main reason why so few BASIC programmers have "jumped ship" to C in the past is BASIC is the first language learned by nearly all non-professional programmers.

But now that you have an ST, you should change to C as soon as possible. Although ST BASIC is a highly refined language, it does not allow you to write more advanced programs.

The main reason for this is that GEM is inaccessable from BASIC. And the fantastic possibilities of GEM and mouse input, the fast MC68000 microprocessor and the ample RAM in the 520 ST or 1040 ST, are the outstanding capabilities of this computer.

For example, if you want to make use of the sophisticated graphics capability of the ST, you must program either in machine language or in C. There are a few graphics commands in ST BASIC, but they just scratch the surface of the fantastic graphics capability of this computer.

It may not make sense to program in machine language on the ST. The speed of C approaches the speed of actual machine language—and it takes 6 to 10 times longer to program in machine language than it does in C. Furthermore, machine language programs are much more difficult to modify than programs written in C.

Another disadvantage of working in machine language is that your machine code programs cannot be easily transported to computers with different processors. Even with the same processors, adaptation to a different computer can be an agonizing process for every programmer. On the other hand, C programs from the ST are easier to transfer to other computers, such as the Commodore *AMIGA* or the IBM PC.

The programs you now run on your ST are therefore more likely to have a future if you write them in C. If you later change to a different computer system at a later time, you can still use your old C programs.

The power of C is demonstrated by the fact that not only GEM, but <u>all</u> of the Digital Research routines not written in machine code were written in C.

This book gives you the opportunity to move from BASIC to C. Although the common difficulties mentioned above do hinder the programmer from changing from BASIC to C, they can all be overcome. To make things easier, the entire concept of this book was developed especially for the BASIC programmer, and is directed specifically toward the capabilities of the ST.

The examples in this book use the Alcyon compiler that is part of the Atari Developer's Package. It was chosen because it is considered the "standard" among ST C compilers. Other C compilers such as Megamax, Lattice, and Mark Williams are very similar and can be used with very few syntax changes.

Chapter 2

First steps for (former) BASIC programmers

First Steps for (former) BASIC programmers

2.1 Learn the elementary structures of C in one day

Yes, it's possible. This chapter includes all of the important structures of C—and you'll need just one day to work through it. You will be able to write your first C programs on the ST by the time you finish this chapter.

We can learn a new programming language only by experimenting with it and writing programs. For this reason you will start writing in C now, so that in a short time you reach a point where you can write your own programs unaided.

You can switch to C quickly and easily by studying this chapter. We'll concentrate on the important language elements without losing ourselves in details, limitations, exceptions, and rules. This chapter makes absolutely no claim to be comprehensive or complete. The details, along with many other essentials (such as tips and tricks for effective programming in C) are found in the subsequent chapters.

With the compact, yet precise introduction in this chapter, we'll have you writing your own C programs in the shortest time possible.

Of course, this method also has its disadvantages. If we leave out complete details for a while, we cannot avoid repeating parts of this chapter later on. However, we believe that this ongoing review is not annoying, but helps you learn even more.

2.2 Functions and text output to the screen

One elementary task in every programming language is displaying comments and messages on the screen. For example, how do you make the computer display:

```
Hello, how are you?
```

on the screen?

In BASIC, we do it with a simple PRINT statement:

```
10 PRINT "HELLO, HOW ARE YOU?"
```

In C, the corresponding program looks similar:

```
main()
{
    printf("Hello, how are you?\n");
    gemdos(0x1);
}
```

The additional GEMDOS call:

```
gemdos(0x1)
```

must be added to the program for the ST's C compiler.

This causes the program execution to stop until a certain key is pressed. You must keep this GEM-specific characteristic in mind with the following examples. Always add the GEMDOS call to the end of your program.

One word about compiling these C programs. Because of the powerful capabilities of the ST, compilation is often quite time-consuming. For instance, a different LINK procedure is used depending on whether the C program is a TOS application, a GEM application or a desk accessory.

In our example program:

```
main()
{
    printf("Hello, how are you?\n");
    gemdos(0x1);
}
```

the first thing we see is the opening:

```
main()
```

This line represents a special C *function*. C programs are normally composed of a series of individual functions.

These functions are somewhat comparable to BASIC subroutines, which are called using GOSUB and ended with RETURN. They also correspond to the procedures familiar to Pascal programmers.

Every function in C is assigned a name. For example, the following function is called input:

```
input()
{
    The commands of the function
    input go here.
}
```

The function called main() is a special function. When the program is executed, main() is always the first function to be called and the first to be carried out. It is therefore the "master function" in the C program.

It is important to make sure that every C program contains a main() somewhere in its text. main() normally makes calls to other functions—additional subprograms.

The braces surrounding the program in our simple example start and end all the statements that make up a function. The last closing brace is like the END command in BASIC.

Now we come to the line:

```
printf("Hello, how are you?\n");
```

To make life simpler, we will say that:

```
printf(    );
```

is equivalent to the `PRINT` command in BASIC, even though `printf` does more and is syntactically more complex than the BASIC command `PRINT`. Text to be printed must be enclosed by parentheses as in our example, like the argument of a function.

Now we'll explain the meaning of the '`\n`' in the program text. This symbol is not printed, but executes a line feed (end-of-line).

If you had left this symbol off and printed the line like this:

```
printf("Hello, how are you?");
```

it would be equivalent to the BASIC instruction:

```
10 PRINT "Hello, how are you?";
```

2.3 Program format

You could also formulate the C program like this:

```
main()
{
    printf("Hello, ");
    printf("how ");
    printf("are ");
    printf("you?");
    printf("\n");
    gemdos(0x1);
}
```

This is also possible in BASIC. The program then reads as follows:

```
10 PRINT "Hello, ";
20 PRINT "how ";
30 PRINT "are ";
40 PRINT "you?";
50 PRINT
```

An essential difference between the C compiler and the BASIC interpreter is that the C compiler accepts an arbitrary program format. This means that you could also write the program as follows:

```
main()
    {
        printf("Hello,
        how
        are
        you?\n");
        gemdos(0x1);
    }
```

Normally a C compiler accepts this input. A BASIC interpreter does not. However, you should not become accustomed to this sort of programming style or the legibility of your programs will suffer. Several compilers, including the Alcyon compiler from the ST Developer's Package, do not accept this format either. Instead you'll get this error message:

```
string cannot cross line
```

Take a look at the semicolons in the C program. Their job is to separate single statements, much like the colon in BASIC or the separating semicolon in Pascal.

2.4 Numerical screen output

We have now had our first experience with program format, looked at functions, and learned how to print text on the screen. But printing numeric variables to the screen is not as easy.

Numeric output as well as simple text output is possible in BASIC using a
`PRINT` command. Take the following BASIC program, for example:

```
10 A=1
20 B=3.14
30 PRINT A;B
40 END
```

The corresponding C program reads as follows:

```
main()
{
    int a;
    float b;
    a = 1;
    b = 3.14;
    printf("%7d %5.1f\n", a, b);
    gemdos(0x1);
}
```

2.4.1 Variable declarations

First, we need a few elementary explanations of the structure of a function in C.

All variables within these routines must be *declared* at the beginning of the function. In BASIC, this is usually not necessary.

The declaration tells the computer which variables it should use and thereby defines the variable names. In this case, they are a and b.

In addition, the variable *types* are established:

```
int a;
```

The variable a therefore represents an integer number, determined by the variable type `int`.

The declaration:

```
float b;
```

establishes b as a floating point variable.

2.4.2 Initializing variables

After initialization, variables must be given a value. In our example program, this process looks like this:

```
a = 1;
b = 3.14;
```

This may appear strange and unnecessarily complicated to BASIC programmers. When you programmed in BASIC in the past, all the variables were automatically set to zero when the program was RUN.

However, this does *not* happen in C. The initial declaration does not assign a value to the variables.

Variables must always be assigned a value explicitly. To the BASIC programmer this may seem unnecessary, but you will find that your C programs are more structured, execute better, and are more easily modified as a result.

2.4.3 The format instructions

Now we come to the program line:

```
printf("%7d  %5.1f\n", a, b);
```

This compares to the following BASIC instruction:

```
PRINT A; B
```

The C statement looks much more complicated. However, it can do much more than you see at first glance.

You already know the basic structure of the `printf` command from our earlier examples.

The only new elements are the control instructions between the quotation marks. These act as format instructions. One example of this is the format:

```
"%5.1f"
```

Every format statement is prefixed with a % character. This lets the computer know that it should output a value (here the value of the variable b) in a specific format.

The format itself is determined by the element 5.1. The 5.1 means that the number should be printed in a space comprised of five characters and containing one place after the decimal.

The letter f, an abbreviation of "float", indicates the conversion element and instructs the ST to print out a floating-point number. Correspondingly, the d stands for an integer (whole number) value. Format statements are quite useful. Output formatting in BASIC is considerably more complicated than it is in C with the `printf` command.

2.5 Loops and comments

We cannot write very meaningful programs using only text and numeric output. We also need *loops*, like the FOR-NEXT loop in BASIC.

2.5.1 The `for` loop

You should have an easy time understanding the `for` loop in C, because it's closely related to the FOR-NEXT loop in BASIC. You'll notice this right away in the following example program. The program prints a list of the numbers from one to twenty and their squares:

```
main()
{
    int x;
    for (x = 1; x <= 20; x = x + 1)
        printf("%2d %3d\n", x, x*x);
    gemdos(0x1);
}
```

The program output looks like this:

```
 1    1
 2    4
 3    9
 4   16
 5   25
 6   36
 7   49
 8   64
 9   81
10  100
 .
 .
 .
18  324
19  361
20  400
```

The corresponding BASIC commands are clearly similar to C's for loop:

```
10 FOR X=1 TO 20 STEP +1
20     PRINT X; X*X
30 NEXT X
40 END
```

The result of this BASIC program is absolutely identical to that of the previous C program.

We already know the structure of the C program. First, the function main() is opened and the variable x must be declared as an integer. Then comes the actual for loop:

```
for (x = 1; x <= 20; x = x + 1)
    printf("%2d %3d\n", x, x*x);
```

The first thing done is to set the first x value to one. The BASIC construction:

```
FOR X=1
```

becomes the following in C:

```
x = 1;
```

Note that it is not necessary to give the variable x a value beforehand under these circumstances. An additional x = 1; is not necessary before the for loop. The initialization takes place right in the loop instead.

The second part of the C for loop is the *outer interval limit*.

The BASIC FOR-NEXT expression:

```
TO 20
```

is replaced in C with:

```
x <= 20;
```

Many other delimiters are possible, of course. One example would be:

    x < 21;

which has exactly the same effect as the instruction x <= 20.

The third part of the `for` loop is the step width. In BASIC, you don't have to include the step width of +1.

When you omit the STEP instruction from a FOR-NEXT loop, the BASIC interpreter automatically sets the step width to +1.

You must change your thinking a little in C, however. The step width must always be specified explicitly, as it is in this case with:

    x = x + 1

This is comparable to the BASIC instruction:

    STEP +1

Note also that the loop declaration may not be followed by a semicolon:

    for(first interval bound;
            second bound;
                step width)

You've probably noticed that we have always talked about the `for` loop in relation to a BASIC FOR-NEXT loop. But where do we find the corresponding NEXT statement in a C program? In other words, how many statements does the C compiler repeat within the `for` loop?

The answer is simple: one. If we want to repeat more than one statement, we can place them in braces, making a statement block.

This is an example:

```c
main()
{
    int x;
    for (x = 1; x <= 20; x = x + 1)
        {
            printf("Value of X is...");
            printf("%2d\n", x);
            printf("X squared is  ...");
            printf("%3d\n", x*x);
        }
    gemdos(0x1);
}
```

Here, a whole block of `printf` calls follows the `for` statement. The entire block must be enclosed in braces.

This program prints the values of x together with the values of x squared, each printed on a separate line:

```
Value of X is ... 1
X squared is  ... 1

Value of X is ... 2
X squared is  ... 4

    (through)

Value of X is ... 20
X squared is  ... 400
```

2.5.2 The `while` loop

This loop is probably less familiar to you as a BASIC programmer than the `FOR-NEXT` loop. For our purposes, `while` can best be expressed as "as long as."

The algorithm of the loop used in our previous example program should look something like this:

```
x = 1;
as long as x <= 20 do the following:
{
    x = x + 1;
    print x
    and x squared
}
```

You can also formulate this algorithm in BASIC like this:

```
10 X=1
20 '
30 IF X<=20 THEN PRINT X;X*X:GOTO30
40 '
50 END
```

Below is the corresponding C program with the correct syntax for the while loop:

```
/* Value table for X squared */
main()
{
    int x;
    x = 1;
    while (x <= 20)
    {
        printf("Value of X is ...");
        printf("%2d\n", x);
        printf("X squared is   ...");
        printf("%3d\n", x*x);
        x = x + 1;
    }
        gemdos(0x1);
}
```

This program prints out a value table just like our last example, which used a for loop.

However, you must initialize x with a value after you declare it as an integer. This was done in our program with:

    x = 1;

This is important, because the x value is used immediately as a loop condition. In the `for` loop, the initialization is handled right in the loop declaration.

The syntax of the `while` loop is self-explanatory. The parentheses enclose the condition for the execution of the statements in the loop. The instructions to be repeated are enclosed in the braces. This corresponds exactly to the syntax of the `for` loop.

For example, if only one instruction needs to be repeated, the braces can be dropped, just as they are in our `for` loop example. Also parallel to the `for` loop syntax is the fact that no semicolon follows the `while` loop declaration.

The step width must be handled inside the loop instruction, as it is in this case with:

    x = x + 1;

We also could have specified any other step width, such as "2" or "0.5".

2.5.3 Comments in C

The only thing missing now is an explanation of the first program line:

    /* Value table for X squared */

This command corresponds to a REM line in BASIC. You could add the corresponding BASIC line to the previous BASIC program:

    5 REM Value table for X squared

The text between the slashes and asterisks is ignored by the compiler.

To maintain the readability of long programs, you should learn early to insert comments about the structure at the beginning of your functions (subroutines).

The syntax of this instruction is always as follows:

```
/* Comment text */
```

Note that a semicolon may not follow a comment line.

2.6 Data input

At this point you're ready to write your first programs. But there is still one very important element missing: the ability to enter data.

Just as the `printf` instruction can do much more than the normal BASIC `PRINT` instruction, there are many different variations of data input with different capabilities in C.

To keep things simple, we'll first simulate the BASIC `INPUT` command with two different C commands.

2.6.1 The `getchar()` function

The syntax of our first input option reads like this:

```
letter = getchar()
```

This function, which assigns a character read from the keyboard to the variable letter, makes it easy to enter a single character in a running program. It is comparable to a BASIC routine containing a GET command:

```
10 LET LT$ =""
20 GET LT$
30 IF LT$="" THEN GOTO 20
40 '
50 REM LETTER LT$ CHOSEN
```

Longer character strings must be built-up using a repeat loop. It can look like the following in C:

```
#include "stdio.h"
main()
{
int Lt;
    Lt = getchar();
    while (Lt != EOF)

        {
            printf("%c\n", l);
            Lt = getchar();
        }
    gemdos(0x1);
}
```

The program takes the characters from the keyboard and prints them on the screen. The input is ended with <Control>Z.

The variable `l` is declared as type integer. This may seem strange to a BASIC programmer. You may think you should have to declare a character type, because a character is printed out.

`getchar()` doesn't really read a character from the keyboard, but the ASCII value of the character. This value must be passed as type `int` rather than type `char`.

Of course, `l` can also be defined as a character value. The program would run perfectly in almost every situation. But problems can sometimes arise in actual practice. It is therefore better to use integer values instead of character values with the `getchar()` function.

The expression "%c" in this `printf` call tells the computer to print a character.

Another new thing here is the EOF. This means End Of File. It indicates when the input was ended—in other words, when <RETURN> was entered.

One further comment: != in C stands for "is not equal to." It corresponds to the BASIC inequality operator <>.

The command

```
#include "stdio.h"
```

combines the standard library of the compiler with the program. This defines a set of standard functions and constants. In our example, these are the EOF constant and the function getchar().

2.6.2 The Alcyon C `getchar()`

A change is necessary to the Alcyon C compiler included in the Atari development system. This version does not have a working getchar() function. It must be implemented with a separate function.

To do this, add the following lines to the previous program:

```
getchar()
{
    char c;
    return((read(0, &c, 1) > 0) ? c & 0377 : EOF);
}
```

This function addition must be made to all programs that use the getchar() function.

At the time this book is being published, it is not certain whether or not the function is implemented in the official Alcyon C ST version.

On the ST, the signal for the end of a line is <Control>Z. To end the program, you must use this control character instead of <RETURN>.

The output for our program using the Alcyon C package can look like this:

    abcd^Z

The output would then read:

    a
    b
    c
    d

You don't have to worry about this function anymore for the time being.

2.6.3 The `scanf` function

You can now input single characters into the computer. This is very easy to do, as you have already seen.

But this is not enough, obviously. We will now find ways to implement the BASIC commands like `INPUT A` or `INPUT A$` in C.

Let's translate the following BASIC program:

```
10 INPUT A% : REM INTEGER NUMBERS ONLY
20 '
30 END
```

In C, we get:

```
main()
{
    int a;
    scanf("%d", &a);
    gemdos(0x1);
}
```

Note the ampersand (&) in front of the a variable. This is necessary whenever numeric input is entered with the `scanf` function.

This involves a *pointer*, which tells the computer where input is to be stored. We'll look at pointers in more detail later.

2.6.4 The Alcyon C `scanf()`

Alcyon C stores ASCII inputs, and therefore the `scanf()` function stores the input as files, each with a line feed at the end. A <Control>Z (0x1a) stands for the `End Of File`.

The input for `scanf()` must therefore be ended with this control code. This is not enough for the input to be accepted, however. A character which does not match the format must be entered before the terminating <Control>Z. The reason for this is that the `scanf()` function terminates as soon as the input does not agree with the format. For example, the input of the integer 1245 must be written as follows:

```
1245_^Z
```

The space (_) doesn't match the input, since it doesn't represent a number. The ^Z represents the terminating <Control>Z character. <Return> must be pressed after this input.

This complicated input procedure is unacceptable for the user. We hope that an updated version of the Alcyon C for the ST will provide a standard input ended simply with <RETURN>.

2.6.5 Further use of variables in programs

Now let's explore the further use of the `&a` variables in a program.

Our BASIC program, which uses the variable `A%` after input, might look like the following:

```
10 INPUT A%
20 PRINT A%; A%^2
30 END
```

Translated into C it reads:

```
main()
{
    int a;
    scanf("%d", &a);
    printf("%d %d\n", a, a * a);
    gemdos(0x1);
}
```

The address operator `&` is used here only with the `scanf` instruction.

2.7 Arithmetic in C

As a BASIC programmer, you should have no trouble learning how to use arithmetic expressions in C, because in many respects it is almost identical to BASIC arithmetic.

2.7.1 Similarities to BASIC

In our previous examples we presented the math as self-explanatory, without explaining it in any detail.

A few examples of what we've used so far are:

1. x = x + 1;
2. x * x;
3. while(x <= 20)
4. for(x = 1; x <= 20; x = x + 1)
5. a = 2/(3*3);

Here you see once again that C expressions like a=2/(3*3) are identical to BASIC expressions in their syntax, logic, and placement of parentheses.

In addition, all of the following C operations correspond to their BASIC counterparts:

```
<, >, <=, >=, +, *, /,
```

2.7.2 Differences from BASIC

But C has minor notation differences which often trip up BASIC programmers. One specific example has already been covered. The inequality operator, represented in BASIC with this:

```
<>
```

is written in C using:

```
!=
```

C also distinguishes between:

```
=
```

for value assignment, and

```
==
```

which is the equality operator. The symbol for value assignment, as used in the following line:

```
x = -1;
```

assigns a value to x, just as in BASIC.

An `if` statement (see the next section) is implemented with an expression such as:

```
if (x == 1)
    statement
```

C uses the equivalence operator == to test for the equality of two values.

There are still a few more formal differences.

In BASIC, the logical

> AND

is formulated in C with:

> &&

Similarly, BASIC's logical

> OR

is represented in C with:

> ||

The BASIC line:

```
IF A=1 AND B=2 OR C=5 THEN (...)
```

is translated in C as:

```
if(a == 1 && b == 2 || c == 5)
{
    ...
}
```

At first glance, this looks somewhat unusual. However, all that is new is the form of some of the arithmetic expressions in C. You already know the syntax and possible uses of these expressions from BASIC, and there are no major changes.

2.7.3 The increment and decrement operators

In C, there are instructions like:

```
x++;        (or)        ++x;
```

These lines use an element called an *increment operator*. This operator increments the value of x by one. We'll learn what the difference between the two forms is in a later section.

The following statement:

```
x++;
```

is equivalent (by itself) to the BASIC-like statement:

```
x = x + 1;
```

In the same way, the *decrement operator* (--) allows us to use the statement:

```
x--
```

in place of:

```
x = x - 1
```

The increment and decrement operators are unusual in that they can be used either before or after the variable they modify, and have different operations in each case. Since they are operators, their result is an expression. More on this later.

2.8 More control structures in C

Control structures define the execution order of commands within a program. We have already covered two such structures, the `for` and `while` loops.

Now, we'll quickly cover the `if` and `if-else` control structures and make ourselves familiar with them.

2.8.1 The `if` statement

The following BASIC program asks you to guess a number, and prints an appropriate message if you guess the right one. It shouldn't be taken too seriously—its main purpose is to demonstrate the `if` structure.

```
10 INPUT X%
20 '
30 IF X%=13 THEN PRINT "CORRECT!":
   PRINT "THAT WAS THE ANSWER!"
40 END
```

When we translate this program into C, we get:

```
main()
{
    int x;
    scanf("%d", &x);

    if (x == 13)
        {
            printf("Correct!\n");
            printf("That was the answer!\n");
        }
    gemdos(0x1);
}
```

As you can see, there are really no differences in the normal `if` structure for the BASIC programmer. The construction is the same, and the syntax corresponds to the `while` loop, which we've already covered.

Note especially the comparison (x == 13). Unlike BASIC, it uses two equal signs in a row. Also note that no semicolon follows the `if` command.

If more than one statement follows the `if` condition, as in our example, they must all be surrounded by braces.

However, they can be left off if only one command is to be executed after the `if` statement.

2.8.2 The `if-else` statement

Most versions of BASIC allow IF-THEN-ELSE control structures. If we were to add ELSE statement to the above program, we would get:

```
10  INPUT X%
20  '
30  IF X%=13 THEN PRINT "VICTORY!":
    PRINT "THAT WAS THE ANSWER!"
    ELSE PRINT "TOO BAD! WRONG GUESS!"
40  END
```

Our extended C program then looks like this:

```
main()
{
    int x;
    scanf("%d", &x);
    if (x == 13)
        {
            printf("Correct!\n");
            printf("That was the answer!\n");
        }
    else
        {
            printf("Too bad! Wrong guess!");
            printf("\n");
        }
    gemdos(0x1);
}
```

Just as in BASIC, the `else` statement is simply placed after the `if`.

However, it's very easy to formulate a large block of commands directly as an `else` statement. But in BASIC, where all `ELSE` commands must fit onto one line, this is not possible without additional programming. The only real solution is to call a subroutine with `GOSUB`. For a single call this is neither as elegant nor as efficient as the C method for a single call, however.

The syntax of the `else` statement should be clear and self-explanatory now that you've had some exposure to C control structures. Just as with the `if` and `while` statements, there is no semicolon after the `else` statement.

Again, `else` causes one statement to be executed if the result of the `if` statement is false. If more than one statement is to be executed, they must be placed in braces.

2.9 Data types in C

2.9.1 Variables

You have already learned the most important variable types:

   `int`   for integer numbers

   `float` for floating-point numbers

   `char`   for character values

C has more variable types for other purposes, such as greater mathematical precision. We will cover these other types in later chapters.

2.9.2 Constants

C can also define *symbolic constants*. This is done with the `#define` instruction. It might look like this in a program:

```
#define INCREMENT 1
#define LO.BOUND 0
#define HI.BOUND 20
main()
{
    int x;
    for(x = LO.BOUND; x <= HI.BOUND; x = x + INCREMENT)
        printf("%2d\n", x);
    gemdos(0x1);
}
```

This short C program counts from the lower bound of an interval (defined with the value zero by the constant `LO.BOUND`) until the upper bound `HI.BOUND` is reached. The increment is set at one.

The three constants defined before the main program are used later in the `for` statement. You might ask why we even bother with symbolic constants. Granted, in this short program they are somewhat complicated and really unnecessary.

Constants are much more useful in larger programs. If there are values which you use over and over in a program and they do not change, you should define them as constants. This way, if you want to change this value, you only have to change it once instead of every occurrence.

The structure of a constant definition is:

```
#define CONSTANT contents
```

You should note that no semicolon follows the `#define` construction, just as none follows a comment. You can assign text to a symbolic constant as well as numbers. The compiler then converts the constant text during compiling, and replaces all of the constant names with the corresponding text. As you would expect, constant names within quotes are not replaced.

2.9.3 Arrays

Arrays in C are very much like arrays in BASIC, so there's nothing to be afraid of here.

The BASIC dimensioning command:

```
10 DIM S(20)
```

is accomplished in C with the variable declaration:

```
int s[20]      (or)      float s[20]
```

or any other variable type that the elements of the array are to have.

Note that unlike most BASIC arrays, which start at 1, arrays in C start numbering the elements with zero. This means that int s[20] dimensions an array with a total of 20 elements, which are then numbered s[0] through s[19].

An important point for BASIC programmers is that every single element in an array must be given a value before it is used. The BASIC command:

```
DIM S(20)
```

automatically sets all of the variables from S(1) to S(20) to zero. But in C, you must do this separately before you can do anything else with the array. In the following example a short for loop does this job:

```
main()
{
    int s[20];
    int i;
    for(i = 0; i < 20; i = i + 1)
        s[i] = 0;
        /* additional program steps... */
    gemdos(0x1);
}
```

In this program, the variables from s[0] to s[19] in the array are initialized and ready for further use.

For practice, here is a short program that uses the getchar() function to read a character from the keyboard and put it into the array. In BASIC, it would look like this:

```
10  DIM T$(50)
20  I=0
30  A$=""
40  GET A$
50  IF A$="" THEN 40
60  '
70  I=I+1
80  T$(I)=A$
90  IF A$<>CHR$(13) AND I<50 THEN GOTO 30
100 END
```

The C version follows:

```c
#define EOF (-1)
main()
{
    char a;
    int i;
    char t[50];
    for(i = 0; i < 50; i = i + 1)
        t[i] = 0;
    i = 0;
    a = getchar();
    while (a != EOF && i < 50)
        {
            i = i + 1;
            t[i] = a;
            a = getchar();
        }
    printf("Contents of the string:\n");
    for (i = 0; i < 50; ++i)
        printf("%c\n", t[i]);
    gemdos(0x1);
}
getchar()
{
    char c;
    return((read(0, &c, 1) >0) ? c & 0377 :EOF );
}
```

All of the structures in this program have already been explained in the section on data input and the `getchar()` function.

Something new here is the string assignment section. The syntax and details of arrays were explained on the preceding pages.

You should not only read the above program, but also type it into the computer. You should also experiment with the C you have learned so far by changing or expanding the program. You'll learn C like any other language, through active programming and practical application—**not** by just reading! This advice applies to all of the programs in this book.

Chapter 3

The basic elements of C

The BASIC elements of C

Now that you've learned the elementary structures of C, you're ready to write your first solo programs.

First you should solidify your knowledge of C. This means that you should experiment—sit in front of the ST and write simple programs based on what you learned in the previous chapter. The time that you so invest now will be worth twice its value later, when we work through the more complex structures of C.

To help you with your first programs, the following pages contain a short review of the material we have covered so far, with special emphasis on comparisons to BASIC.

3.1 Program structure

A program consists of individual *functions*. Every function has a *title* and its instructions are enclosed in braces.

Example:

```
square()
{
     instructions in the function "square"
}
```

The function with the title `main()` has a special position. It is always the first function to be executed and it usually calls the other functions. Each individual *statement* within a function is separated from the others by a semicolon, in the same manner that BASIC commands on a single line can be separated by colons.

3.2 Comments

Comments help to explain your program to both yourself and other programmers. Comments are ignored by the C compiler. Their syntax is as follows:

```
/* Comment text—can contain anything */
```

3.3 Screen output

Strings are printed on the screen as follows:

```
printf("Text");
```

This example does not create a carriage return—that is, additional output would follow immediately after "Text" and not on a new line. To create a carriage return, a command character must be added to the end of the text:

```
printf("Text\n");
```

Numerical output requires an indication of the *variable type* and follows a format like the following:

```
printf("%d %f7.2\n" a,b);
```

The most important variable type instructions are:

- **d** for integer output
- **f** for floating-point output
- **s** for string output

The format "7.2" in the above example of the printf instruction causes a number with a total of 7 digits, including two after the decimal point, to be printed out for the variable b.

3.4 Variables and constants

Constants are defined using the `#define` construction before the `main()` function in a program, and they can be used in every function thereafter.

Example:

```
#define constant 33
```

No semicolon follows the definition.

Variables used within a function must be defined before they are used. The most important variable types are as follows:

```
int a;     definition for an integer.
float a;   definition for a floating-point number.
char a;    a represents a single character.
```

All variable types can be defined as *arrays*. For example, this is how an array of 20 integers is defined:

```
int a[20]
```

All variables, as well as all individual elements of an array, must always be given a value before they are used in any way. If you have defined the variable a as an integer, then a variable assignment such as the following must take place:

```
a = 1;
```

3.5 Loops

The `for` loop is represented in C as follows:

```
for(i = 0; i < 20; i = i + 1)
    statement (block)
```

The three parameters give the initial value of the *initial loop value, end value,* and *step size.*

Multiple loop instructions must be enclosed in braces. This is not necessary for only one instruction. No semicolon follows the `for` statement (unless the loop is empty).

The `while` loop has the following syntax:

```
while(x < 15)
    {
        Commands to be repeated
        x = x + 1;
    }
```

The increment is specified within the loop. In the example above, it is set to one with:

```
x = x + 1;
```

3.6 Data input

Single characters can be read using the `getchar()` function, similar to the BASIC command GET:

```
int a;
a = getchar();
```

The `scanf` command can be substituted for the BASIC `INPUT` command:

```
int a;
scanf("%d", &a);
```

Just like the `printf` command, `scanf` must use one or more of the variable types, of which `%d`, `%f`, and `%s` are the most important. In the `scanf` command, the address operator `&` must always precede the variable name, unless the variable is an array name, such as a string.

3.7 Arithmetic in C

The BASIC inequality operator `<>` translates to `!=` in C.

The logical AND is represented by `&&`, and the OR by `||`.

The statement x=x+1 can be rewritten using the *increment operator* ++ as x++ or ++x. Similarly, the expression x=x-1 can be rewritten with the *decrement operator* -- as x-- or --x.

3.8 The `if-else` control structure

The `if-else` structure has the following syntax:

```
if(x == 1)
    {
        then execute these commands
    }
else
    {
        execute these commands.
    }
```

It is important that no semicolon follows the `if` and `else` statements, and that a double equals sign (==) is used for comparison:

```
if(x == 1)
```

This concludes our brief overview of the fundamental elements of C.

This list is certainly not complete, because C has many more elements than those mentioned so far.

Use this list to start programming. You can learn C only through practice!

Chapter 4

Screen Input/Output Operations

Screen Input/Output operations

The following chapters take a close look at various operations of C, explaining them with numerous examples from BASIC. The information will help you learn C's details, as well as the powerful C structures.

Now that you have already learned a few elementary capabilities of data input and output, we'll give you a detailed description of these operations on the screen.

4.1 Outputting text on the screen

We have already covered text output in the previous chapters. First we'll review briefly:

The BASIC line:

```
10 PRINT "HELLO"
```

would be translated into C as follows:

```
main()
{
    printf("Hello\n");
    gemdos(0x1);
}
```

The control character \n is the new-line character. It moves subsequent output to the start of the next line. If this character is omitted:

```
main()
{
        printf("he");
        printf("llo");
}
```

then no new-line character is generated.

This assembles the word "hello" from two words. It corresponds to the following example in BASIC:

```
10 PRINT "he";
20 PRINT "llo";
```

In both cases, the output is as follows:

```
hello_
```

The underline character (_) represents the cursor position after the execution of the command.

4.2 Printing numerical values

In the previous chapters we saw that printing numerical values in C is more flexible than in BASIC, but that it is also more difficult.

The BASIC routine:

```
10 X=3.14
20 PRINT X
```

translates into C as:

```
main()
{
    float x;
        x = 3.14;
        printf("%f\n", x);
    gemdos(0x1);
}
```

If we wanted to print integers instead of 3.14, we would write a BASIC program like this:

```
10 X%=15
20 PRINT X%
```

The corresponding C program would read:

```
main()
{
    int x;
        x = 15;
        printf("%d\n", x);
    gemdos(0x1);
}
```

We could use an even shorter program to get the same result:

```
10 PRINT 15
```

The corresponding C function looks like this:

```
main()
{
    printf("%d\n", 15);
    gemdos(0x1);
}
```

The complete syntax definition of the `printf` function is as follows:

   printf("*format statements*", *argument 1*, *argument 2*, ...);

The format statements contain commands that determine the form of the output. In our examples, the specification `%d` was chosen for the integer 15, just as `%f` was chosen for the floating point value `3.14`. In the next section we'll look at these conversion specifications more closely.

4.3 Format instructions

These commands can be divided into the *format specifiers*, which determine how many places of a number are printed, for example, and the *conversion elements*, which determine the output type, such as integer, float, or string. First we'll look at the conversion elements.

4.3.1 Conversion elements

You are already familiar with these conversion characters:

       f   for floating point numbers, such as 3.14

       d   for integers, such as 15

We also briefly mentioned the conversion character:

       s   for character output

However, C has some more type declarations that we left out of our initial overview. The next sections contain a complete list of the conversion characters which the `printf` function allows.

4.3.1.1 Numerical output

%d   As in the examples, this character is used to print decimal numbers. If you try to output a floating-point number with this conversion character, you will get an error. This is a very common mistake and happens most often when an expression which does not return an integer is used.

%u   Similar to %d, except the integer is treated as unsigned (always positive).

%o   Prints the argument in base 8 (octal) without the leading zero.

%x   Works like %o, except that it puts the argument into base 16 (hexadecimal).

%f   Outputs `float` or `double` (floating-point numbers with double precision) arguments. The values are printed out in decimal form (with leading minus sign if necessary).

%e   Similar to %f in that it applies to `float` and `double` variable types, but the resulting output is in exponential (scientific) notation:

    (-)m.nnnnnnE(+-)xx

%g   Results in output like %e or %f, whichever is shorter.

4.3.1.2 Character output

%c   Treats the output as a single character.

%s   Prints a string, i.e. an array of characters. Every position of the string that has been given a character value is printed out.

4.3.2 Format specifiers

In a `printf` call the format specifiers tell how many places before and after the decimal point will be printed, and also whether the output will be right- or left-justified.

Some formats have default values:

%f   Places six digits after the decimal point, while the number of digits before the decimal point remains arbitrary.

%e   Sets number of digits after the decimal point to six, in exponential notation.

If you want to change these formats or set other formats, a statement of the following form can be used:

    "%7.5f"

This prints a floating-point number with a total of seven digits, five of which are after the decimal point.

Positioning the output:

If a minus sign directly follows the % sign, then the text or variable will be left-justified. The normal alignment, without the added minus sign, is right-justification. These rules apply only when the argument to be printed is smaller than the defined field width. If the argument will not fit into the field when printed, the argument will be extended to the left, with the numbers filling in from the right.

4.3.3 Examples of numeric output

For the moment we'll concentrate on outputting numbers to the screen. Let's take the following BASIC program line as an example:

    10 PRINT 2*13

Translated to C, we get:

```
main()
{
    printf("%d\n", 2*13);
    gemdos(0x1);
}
```

Just like with BASIC, we can carry out a calculation right in the output line instead of printing just a single number.

This also applies for a succession of calculations, as in the following BASIC program:

    10 PRINT 2*13; 2/3; 3.14*2.222222; 4-2.2

We would write the following C function:

```
main()
{
    printf("%d %f %f %f\n", 2 * 13, 2.0 / 3.0;
           3.14 * 2.222222, 4.0 - 2.2);
    gemdos(0x1);
}
```

We can so the same with variables in calculations.

The BASIC program:

```
10 A=6
20 B=88
30 '
40 PRINT A/B
```

is translated in C as:

```
main()
{
    float a,
          b;
    a = 6;
    b = 88;
    printf("%f\n", a/b);
    gemdos(0x1);
}
```

Here there are really no essential differences between the two versions.

Look closely at the variable declaration. You should make sure that you do not create a new format as a result of calculations. This can happen when a floating-point number results from two integer variables. When this happens, the format must be changed to %f to avoid an errors or incorrect output.

4.3.4 Text formatting

You can format text as well as numbers. Concrete examples are the best way to show how this works.

The printed text is of type `string`, and contains the twelve characters of the name "Fred Johnson".

Format Command	Result
%10s	Fred Johnson
%-10s	Fred Johnson
%20s	--------Fred Johnson
%-20s	Fred Johnson--------
%20.9s	-----------Fred John
%-20.9s	Fred John-----------
%.4s	Fred
%.7s	Fred Jo

4.3.5 More uses for conversions and formats

If we display a normal `float` variable on the screen, as with this program:

```
main()
{
    float a;
    a = 15;
    printf("%f\n", a);
    gemdos(0x1);
}
```

then we get the output 15.000000. The six zeros are printed automatically because we didn't specify any additional format instructions after the % sign.

This format can be improved with a statement like:

```
printf("%.0f\n", a);
```

This statement truncates all positions after the decimal point.

If you want to leave two positions after the decimal point, then the `printf` call would look like this:

```
printf("%.2f\n", a);
```

You should be aware of a very common error associatied with the `%f` format. Look at the following BASIC line:

```
10 PRINT 2/3
```

And now the corresponding C program:

```
main()
{
    printf("%f\n", 2/3);
    gemdos(0x1);
}
```

This produces incorrect output with the result `0.000000`.

In BASIC, the numbers 2 and 3 are automatically handled as floating-point numbers rather than integers during division. This is not the case in C; we must change the program as follows to get the correct answer:

```
main()
{
    printf("%f\n", 2.0/3.0);
    gemdos(0x1);
}
```

The result of this program is now correct:

```
0.666667
```

4.4 Printing string variables on the screen

We have already gone into some detail about printing numeric variables. Now we'll look more closely at printing string variables. One example is the following BASIC program:

```
10 A$="ATARI ST"
20 PRINT A$
```

In C it looks like this:

```
main()
{
    char *a;
    a = "ATARI ST";
    printf("%s\n", a);
    gemdos(0x1);
}
```

The string variable a must be preceded by an indirection operator (*), which is the inverse of the & operator which accompanies the scanf command. In this case, the string variable type %s must be used for output.

The program could have been shortened to:

```
main()
{
    printf("%s\n", "ATARI ST");
    gemdos(0x1);
}
```

Now we will combine two different variable types in our output. Again we start with a BASIC program:

```
10 A%=12345
20 B$="THE NUMBER IS...>"
30 '
40 PRINT B$;A%
```

And now the C version:

```
main()
{
    int a;
    char *b;
    a = 12345
    b = "The number is...>";
    printf("%s %d\n", b, a);
    gemdos(0x1);
}
```

This program has exactly the same output as the BASIC version. The variables a and b were defined as integer and string, respectively, and were subsequently assigned values.

Note the space between the format expressions %s and %d. Because this space is inside quotation marks, it is printed out. This means that an actual space ends up between the string and the number. In BASIC, this separation is automatically performed in the expression:

```
40 PRINT A$;B
```

simply because of the sequence of variables. In C this is generally accomplished by means of an inserted space. Any other text appearing in the control specification for printf will also be printed out.

Let's look at this more closely in another program:

```
10 T$="USER"
20 PRINT "HELLO ";T$
```

Now the C program:

```
main()
{
    char *t;
    t = "user";
    printf("Hello %s\n", t);
    gemdos(0x1);
}
```

In this example, it is easy to see that all of the characters (not belonging to a conversion specifier) inside the quotation marks are printed out. Most interesting is that in the call

```
printf("Hello %s\n", t);
```

`printf` is able to distinguish between arbitrarily intermixed text and format statements.

This can be seen if you decide to print the variable before the text. This is done by changing the `printf` line to this:

```
printf("%s Hello\n",t);
```

The output is then:

```
user Hello
```

The space before `Hello` is also printed out.

4.4.1 Printing a single character

Unlike BASIC, C distinguishes between individual characters and strings.

The BASIC program:

```
10 T$="W"
20 PRINT T$
```

looks like this in C:

```
main()
{
    char t;
    t = 'W';
    printf("%c\n", t);
    gemdos(0x1);
}
```

Pay attention to the statement:

```
t = 'W';
```

This is the correct syntax for character variables. If t were a string, then the line would be:

```
t = "W";
```

What is the difference between these two lines?

A character variable contains only a single character, which is enclosed in single quotes. However, a string always has an additional control character \0, which indicates the end of the string.

The string in the assignment:

```
t = "W";
```

really consists of W\0 rather than just W.

4.4.2 More screen output

The BASIC function CHR$() is easy to duplicate in C.

The BASIC program line:

```
10 PRINT CHR$(67)
```

is written in C as:

```
main()
{
    printf("%c\n", 67);
    gemdos(0x1);
}
```

This routine prints the character with ASCII value 67 on the screen. This corresponds to the value of the letter C.

The CHR$() instruction is replaced in C by the conversion functions of the printf function.

We can imitate the function ASC("") in much the same way.

The BASIC program:

```
10 PRINT ASC("B")
```

prints the ASCII value of B (66) on the screen.

The corresponding C function reads:

```
main()
{
    printf("%d\n", 'B');
    gemdos(0x1);
}
```

Another, more detailed version is the following:

```
main()
{
    char t;
    t = 'B';
        printf("%d\n", t);
        gemdos(0x1);
}
```

You can use these two functions (i.e. the routines corresponding to ASC and CHR$) to analyze strings or input to see what characters are present, or to eliminate certain characters.

4.4.3 Additional output possibilities

Until now we have used only the printf function to print out data. However, there are two other functions for outputting data.

These functions are:

>putchar() and puts()

What do these functions do? putchar() corresponds directly to the function:

    a = getchar();

We looked at this function in the introductory chapter. You'll remember that this command reads a single character from the keyboard.

In the same manner, putchar() sends a single character to the screen. The use of putchar() is clarified with an example program:

```
#include "stdio.h"
#define putchar(a) putc(a,stdout)
main()
{
    char a;
      a = 'P';
      putchar(a);
    gemdos(0x1);
}
```

This routine assigns the character 'P' to the variable a and prints the single character on the screen.

With putchar() you can print single characters on the screen without the trouble and expense of printf. However, this function is limited to screen output.

Now let's look at the puts() function. This command stands for "output string," and outputs strings of characters.

An example of this is shown with the following BASIC program:

```
10 A$="FRED JOHNSON"
20 PRINT A$
```

This program is easily translated to C with the puts() function:

```
#include "stdio.h"
main()
{
    char *a;
    a = "Fred Johnson";
    puts(a);
    gemdos(0x1);
}
```

For comparison, here is the old formulation with printf:

```
main()
{
    char *a;
    a = "Fred Johnson";
    printf("%s\n", a);
    gemdos(0x1);
}
```

In both examples you can use shorter programs to get the same result, taking as an example the following BASIC line:

```
10 PRINT "P"
```

In C, it can look like this:

```
#include "stdio.h"
#define putchar(c) putc(c,stdout)
main()
{
    putchar('P');
    gemdos(0x1);
}
```

The same program can be written using the standard printf statement:

```
main()
{
    printf("%c\n", 'P');
    gemdos(0x1);
}
```

The same applies to printing strings. The BASIC line:

```
10 PRINT "FRED JOHNSON"
```

is transformed into the C function:

```
#include "stdio.h"
main()
{
    puts("Fred Johnson");
    gemdos(0x1);
}
```

Now compare this to the corresponding `printf` program:

```
main()
{
    printf("%s\n", "Fred Johnson");
    gemdos(0x1);
}
```

As you can see, character output is much more elegant using `putchar()` and `puts()` than it is with `printf()`. In actual programming you will use these compact forms when no conversion formats are necessary. *There is no substitute for the formatting commands supported by the* `printf` *function.*

In addition, when more than one value is to be printed out on a line, only the `printf` function will work, because `puts()` and `putchar()` both execute an automatic new-line.

4.5 Data input functions

In our introductory chapters, we left out quite a bit about input as well as output. In addition to what we have already learned about `scanf` and `getchar()`, there are many other possibilities for data input. Most of all, we need to look more closely at the two input functions we have already learned. First let's examine the function `getchar`.

4.5.1 The `getchar()` function

We have already compared this function to the BASIC GET command. In some BASIC dialects, the INKEY$ function can take the place of GET.

The BASIC programs below:

Version with `INKEY$`:   Version with `GET`:

```
10 A$=INKEY$                    10 GET A$
20 IF A$="" THEN GOTO 10        20 IF A$="" THEN GOTO 10
30 '                            30 '
40 PRINT A$                     40 PRINT A$
```

become the following program in C:

```
#include "stdio.h"
#define getchar() getc(stdin)
#define putchar(c) putc(c,stdout)
main()
{
    int a;
    a = getchar();
    while (a != EOF)
        {
            putchar(a);
            a = getchar();
        }
    gemdos(0x1);
}
```

The specific structures are explained in the introductory chapters. To avoid unnecessary repetition, we will not explain them again. Compare this program with the `getchar()` example in the introductory chapter.

In the formulation chosen here, we have used the `putchar()` function for output and `getchar()` for input of a character. It should be clear to you that these functions are related to each other.

The putchar() syntax reads:

> putchar(*character*);

Similarly, the getchar() structure reads:

> *character* = getchar();

4.5.2 Input with gets()

Along with the putchar() statement for printing a single character, we have the following function that prints a string:

> puts()

There is a corresponding command for data input as well. It is:

> gets(*string*);

gets is an abbreviation for "get string." This function assigns an array of characters—a string—to the variable in the parentheses.

Let's look at a short example:

```
10 INPUT A$
20 PRINT A$
```

This is written in C as follows, using gets() and puts():

```
#include "stdio.h"
main()
{
    char *a;
    gets(a);
    puts(a);
    gemdos(0x1);
}
```

Notice that the output of a string is much more elegant using `puts()`, because this function is much easier to use than the `printf` function. This can be seen by comparing the previous example with the following:

```
#include "stdio.h"
main()
{
    char *a;
    gets(a);
    printf("%s\n", a);
    gemdos(0x1);
}
```

As a result, we conclude:

For reading in single characters or strings, the functions `getchar()` and `gets()` are preferred over the `scanf` function.

Likewise, `putchar()` and `puts()` are preferred for output of characters and strings.

The Alcyon C version in the ST development system has problems with the `gets` function. These are due to an incorrect input format not found in standard C compilers. This function runs with no problem on all other ST C compilers. We hope that the commercial version of the Alcyon C makes use of a standard input format.

4.5.3 The `scanf` input function

This command works not only for the input of numerical values, but also allows the input of strings or single characters. Because of this versatility, the `scanf` function corresponds more closely to the BASIC command INPUT than does any other C function. This versatility is obtained at the cost of a somewhat more complicated structure, however.

The `scanf` function offers the best way to enter numeric data into a program. We will go over each of the two applications separately and in detail in the following pages. First we'll look at the input of characters and strings, and then work with numeric data.

4.5.3.1 scanf for character and string input

The following BASIC program reads in and prints out a string:

```
10 INPUT T$
20 PRINT T$
```

As we have seen, this program can be formulated in C using the `gets()` function, or it can be translated with `scanf`, as in the following program:

```
main()
{
    char *t;
    scanf("%s", t);
    printf("%s\n", t);
    gemdos(0x1);
}
```

We have already declared the variable `t` as a string with the pointer marker `*`. Therefore we need nothing more to specify a pointer in the `scanf` call. It is already a pointer variable. Perhaps you remember that we had to use the pointer marker `&` for numeric input in the `scanf` function. As a general rule, all variables within a `scanf` function call must be pointers.

Another important part of our demo program is the control statement `%s` within the `scanf` call. This tells the ST to output a string expression.

The input format specific to Alcyon C was already explained in the first chapter. The number 15, for example, is entered as follows:

```
15_^Z
```

and strings are ended with <Control>Z:

```
input text^Z
```

4.5.3.2 Arrays in place of pointers

We could also have formulated the program without the pointer variable, as this example demonstrates:

```
main()
{
    char t[30];
    scanf("%s", t);
    printf("%s\n", t);
    gemdos(0x1);
}
```

Here the character variable is declared as an array with 30 elements.

An array is treated like a pointer variable. This means that you can also use arrays in conjunction with `scanf` calls.

Nevertheless, pointer structures are more flexible and use storage more efficiently than array structures. If only twelve elements are placed into a 30-element array, for example, the memory still holds places for 30 elements. However, the pointer structure would have only twelve elements plus an end marker in memory. Thus, a great deal of storage space can be saved by using pointers instead of arrays.

Now, let's look at one more small problem. The BASIC program:

```
10 INPUT "PLEASE TYPE IN THE TEXT "; X$
20 PRINT X$
```

is best translated into C as follows:

```
#include "stdio.h"
main()
{
    char *x;
    printf("Please type in the text ");
    scanf("%s", x);
    puts(x);
    gemdos(0x1);
}
```

In both cases, input directly follows the text without a new-line in between.

4.5.3.3 Entering numbers via `scanf`

The BASIC program:

```
10 INPUT Z%
20 PRINT Z%
```

is translated to C as follows:

```
main()
{
    int z;
    scanf("%d", &z);
    printf("%d\n", z);
    gemdos(0x1);
}
```

So far nothing is new. As we have already learned, the address operator & is always necessary so that the computer knows where it must store the value in memory.

Now let's write a program that allows floating-point numbers as well as integers. In BASIC this is very easy to do:

```
10 INPUT Z
20 PRINT Z
```

And here is the program in C:

```
main()
{
    float z;
    scanf("%f", &z);
    printf("%f\n", z);
    gemdos(0x1);
}
```

This program automatically converts integers to floating-point numbers before assigning them to z.

As we have already learned in the section about formatting, the numbers take a certain format:

```
15.000000
```

The above line is the printed form of the integer 15 in the example. The same section tells how to correct this.

One possibility is the following `printf` statement:

```
printf("%.0f\n", z);
```

which truncates all digits after the decimal point.

4.5.3.4 Entering multiple data

In BASIC it is possible to read in values for several variables with one `INPUT` command:

```
10 INPUT T$, A, B%
20 PRINT T$;A;B%
```

More than one variable can be entered using commas to separate the individual variables in BASIC. And the same is true of C:

```
text, 2, 3.14
```

In C the BASIC program looks like this using a `scanf` call:

```
main()
{
    char *t;
    float a;
    int b;
        scanf("%s %f %d", t, &a, &b);
        printf("%s %f %d", t, a, b);
        gemdos(0x1);
}
```

Both programs do the same thing. In C, the format expressions must be integrated into the `printf` and `scanf` function calls, as we have already seen.

Just as in the `printf` function, the format expressions ("%s %f %d"), separated by spaces, are placed before the variables (t, a, b) which they represent.

4.5.4 The `GET$/INKEY$` function in C

You might complain that we have already covered this with the `getchar()` function. That's true, but the `getchar()` function does not correspond exactly to the BASIC line:

```
10 A$=INKEY$
```

The following expression:

```
character = getchar();
```

does indeed read in a single character, just as the INKEY$ or GET function does in BASIC. But it then expects a RETURN to end the input.

This is not true with the new C function:

```
character = getch();
```

The function `getch` corresponds exactly to the following BASIC routine:

```
10 A$=INKEY$
20 IF A$="" THEN 10
```

When this statement is encountered in a program, execution halts until a key is pressed. The character corresponding to this key is then returned via `getch`.

Used in a program it looks like this:

```
#include "stdio.h"
#define putchar(a) putch(a,stdout)
#define getchar() getc(stdin)
main()
{
    int a;
    a = getch();
    putchar(a);
    gemdos(0x1);
}
char bf[100];
int b=0;
getch()
{
    return((b > 0) ? bf[--b] : getchar());
}
```

Here you see how simple this operation is with the `getch()` function.

However, note that the variable read into `getch()` is of type integer. Just as with the `getchar` function, this function reads in the ASCII value of the character entered—i.e. an integer.

The function call:

```
putchar(a);
```

could have been replaced by this:

```
printf("%c\n", a);
```

4.5.5 Implementing `putchar()`, `getchar()` and `getch()` on Alcyon C for the Atari ST

The compiler version included in the Atari development package does not include the above functions. But they are easy to simulate. The `getchar()` function was already synthesized in the introductory chapter.

If you want to use these functions in Alcyon C, then add the following to the end of your program:

```
/* getchar() */
getchar()
{
    char c;
    return((read(0, &c, 1) > 0) ? c & 0377 : EOF);
}
```

Also, since the `getchar` function is already defined as a macro in `stdio.h`, we have to "undefine" it before our function version will take effect. The new program header must look like this:

```
#include "stdio.h"
#define putchar(a) putch(a,stdout)
#undef getchar
main()
...
```

In Digital C, all input must be ended with a <Control>Z. All of the other C compilers use the traditional C standard, so none of them need this additional control character.

The `putchar()` function can be defined as a macro. All you have to do is insert the following `#define` line before the `main()` in your program:

```
#define putchar(c) putc(c,stdout)
```

The above `getchar` function can also be defined as a macro. This reads:

```
#define getchar() getc(stdin)
```

The function `putch()` can almost always be replaced by `putchar()` and is therefore not constructed here, even though it is also omitted from the Alcyon C function library.

It is not necessary for you to understand the makeup of these functions at this time. In all of the programs in this book, the command extensions are simple enough to be quickly and easily added to the existing programs wherever they are used.

Chapter 5

Variable Types in C

Variable Types in C

Now that we have looked at the screen input/output functions, let's take a closer look at the data types in C. This topic includes explanations of variable names and constants, which we have already touched upon. We'll also cover data types and conversions and declaration headers.

In addition, we'll look at other important areas including arrays and the differences between local and global variables in a program. Finally, we will explain important details and special cases relating to pointers.

5.1 Variable names

In many versions of BASIC, variable names are limited to two characters. Although the names can be longer, only the first two are used to distinguish variables names from each other. There are some exceptions, such as the BASIC on the Sinclair ZX-Spectrum and QL, which allows and identifies variable names of any length.

Normally, however, it is the case that the names:

        VAR_1   and   VAR_2

are seen as the same variable because the first two letters (VA) are the same.

C goes further here and identifies the first *eight* characters of variable names. But just as in BASIC, variable names can be longer than the first eight significant characters.

It it important that the first character of a C variable name be a letter rather than a punctuation mark or a digit. The character "_" counts as a letter for this purpose. It is used most often between words of a variable name to improve readability.

For example, instead of the following variable for a street number:

```
strnum
```

We could use the following name and make the meaning clearer:

```
str_num
```

Another important difference between BASIC and C variable names is that C distinguishes between upper- and lowercase letters. For example, the variable NAME is <u>not</u> the same as the variable name. This is probably the most unusual aspect of C variable names compared to BASIC.

C names do have distinct advantages. In C it has become standard procedure to write the names of symbolic constants in capital letters. By the same token, the names of all other data types are written in lowercase. This leads to substantially better readability in a program, because constants can then be distinguished immediately from variables. You should adopt this practice for your programs as well.

Reserved language elements may never be used as variable names. These elements include:

```
if              else
while           do while
for             switch
case            default
break           continue
return          goto
```

Note also that these language elements generally must be written in lowercase letters.

Choose suggestive variable names, i.e., names that immediately give away the purpose of the name in the program. You'll save yourself a lot of time debugging large programs.

In BASIC you quickly learn to use short variables of one or two characters. You should try to unlearn this when programming in C, especially when working with more complex programs.

5.2 Constants

We developed a program that used symbolic constants in the introductory chapter. As you recall, the definition is made with #define. The full structure reads:

    #define CONSTANT string

There is no semicolon after this declaration.

So far, we have declared only integer constants. However, all variable types can be defined as constants, since the text following the constant name is simply inserted in place of the name where it occurs. Note that this replacement does not occur if the constant name appears in quotation marks as an element of a string.

In the following example program, we define constants for each of the four major variable types in C: INTEGER, FLOAT, CHAR and STRING.

```
#define INTEGER  22
#define FLOAT    1.2345
#define CHAR     'D'
#define STRING   "This is a text"
main()
{
    printf("%d\n", INTEGER);
    printf("%f\n", FLOAT);
    printf("%c\n", CHAR);
    printf("%s\n", STRING);

    gemdos(0x1);
}
```

As you can see, the use of these constants is identical to the use of corresponding variables, despite differing types.

Characters must be enclosed in single quotes. This BASIC expression reads as follows:

    10 CHAR$="D"

The C definition must read:

```
#define CHAR 'D'
```

The equals sign is not necessary in C, and single quotes (') are used instead of double quotes ("). These differences may lead to mistakes because of your familiarity with BASIC. One possible error is this:

```
#define CHAR "D"
```

This error—confusing double and single quotes—can be very frustrating because it is so difficult to find. In addition, this error usually does not generate an error message, but only incorrect output.

From a BASIC standpoint, this statement does not seem to be wrong, because BASIC always uses double quotes. If you take careful note of the small differences between BASIC and C, you will save yourself a good deal of trouble and frustration looking for errors later.

On the other hand, string constants must be enclosed in double quotes, just as with definition of string variables:

```
#define STRING "This is a string"
```

Note that the replacement is strictly text replacement and there are therefore no constant "types." This means that the quotation marks are part of the replacement text.

The `float` constants can also be written out in scientific notation, like this:

```
#define FLOAT 12.65432E-4
```

or like this:

```
#define FLOAT 0.02e5
```

All floating-point constants are handled like `double` variables, i.e. like `float` variables, but with double precision.

Long integer constants can be defined with an L character:

```
12345678L
```

The above is an example of a `long` constant.

An integer that is too large for regular integer format is automatically interpreted as `long`.

5.3 Data types

The elementary data types in BASIC are as follow:

A%	Integer
A	Floating point
A$	Character/string

We will talk about arrays, which are more complex forms of the fundamental data types, in a later section.

The data types above are also found in C. In addition, `double` values are considered one of the elementary data types.

The following list shows the data types which are possible in C:

Data type	Explanation
int	Integer number, no fractional portion
float	Floating-point number with normal precision
double	Floating-point number with double precision
char	One byte, any character from the ST's char. set

Integer variables can be subdivided further. A small diagram will illustrate this:

```
                    ───────────  1.  short int
              ─
    int       ───────────────    2.  long int
              ─
                    ───────────  3.  unsigned int
```

`short int` and `long int` represent integers of varying lengths.

`unsigned int` values are always positive. Unsigned integer values obey the mathematical "modulo 2^n" rules, where n represents the number of bits in an integer value.

Declarations of the integer data types look like this:

```
short int a;
long int b;
unsigned int c;
```

Normally, the word `int` can be left out of the declaration.

At this point, we would like to restate that all declared variables must be given a value before they can be used in a program.

In the following sections we discuss the data types you know from BASIC as strings and arrays.

5.4 Converting data types

In BASIC, variables are not often converted to other variable types. The situation is different in C—data type conversions are very common. We have already mentioned a few of these possibilities.

5.4.1 Character/integer conversion

In the previous chapter, we learned the C equivalent to the BASIC statement:

```
10 PRINT CHR$(66)
```

It reads as follows:

```
main()
{
    printf("%c\n", 66);
    gemdos(0x1);
}
```

The result of both programs is that the character B (ASCII value 66) is printed out on the screen. When you look at the programs closely, you see the same thing is happening in both: the number 66 is being converted to the letter B. But C can do more. The following program is also possible (although it may seem unusual to you as a BASIC programmer):

```
main()
{
    int value;
    value = 123 + 'B';
    printf("%d\n", value);
    gemdos(0x1);
}
```

In the assignment line:

```
value = 123 + 'B';
```

the letter 'B' is automatically converted to the integer corresponding to its ASCII value, and added to 123.

Even more impressive is the following program. It reads in uppercase letters and converts them to lowercase. Other characters are printed out in the same form in which they were read in.

The Atari ST development system version of Alcyon C does *not* perform the conversion of character variables completely. As a result the following program will not run on this compiler. It will, however, run on all other standard compilers.

```c
/* Conversion from upper to lowercase letters */
#include "stdio.h"
#define putchar(c) putc(c,stdout)
main()
{
    int character;
    scanf("%d", &character);
      if (character >= 'A' && character <= 'Z')
          printf("%c\n", character + 'a' - 'A');
      else
          printf("%c\n", character);
    gemdos(0x1);
}
```

It's obvious that the character variable `character` was declared as an integer. In this example it becomes clear how a numeric variable is converted to a character variable. The integer variable is automatically assigned the ASCII value of the character in the `scanf()` function. The character corresponding to this value is then printed on the screen.

When converting characters into numeric values, you must pay attention to whether a negative number results. The C compiler does not check to see if a character value is negative or positive. If a conversion results in the value -30, for example, the compiler would set it to the positive value +30.

It is necessary to declare all variables which are to be assigned by `getchar()` as integers, rather than as characters.

The reason for this is that `getchar()` can be used for all possible inputs. In addition, a separate value for the EOI (End Of Input) is necessary.

This character is treated as a number. Therefore the result of `getchar()` can be outputted only as a number. A character variable usually causes this conversion to be performed.

Now let's sum everything up quickly:

Character and integer values can be combined arbitrarily and used together in arithmetic expressions. This is not possible in BASIC. This aspect of C results in great flexibility, especially when programming character transformations.

5.4.2 Converting between numeric types

If different numeric types are used in an arithmetic expression, the compiler changes them automatically to a single given numeric format. For example, if you use the expression:

```
float_value = integer + float;
```

in a program, where the variable `float_value` of type `float` is being assigned the sum of an integer and a floating-point number, the integer is automatically changed to a floating-point number before the addition occurs.

As in this example, conversions are generally performed only if they make sense.

The following ground rules apply for such transformations:

Initial Variable Type:	Converted to:
short int	int
float	double

If one operand is of the type:	Then the other operand is also converted to the type:
double	double
long	long
unsigned	unsigned

If none of the above is true, the compiler converts all operands to type `integer`.

If you set a `float` variable equal to an integer value, as in the example:

```
float_var = int_var
```

a conversion is performed. The fractional part of `float_var` is suppressed.

Conversions can also be reversed. For example, if you change a character variable into an integer variable and then back into a character variable, no net change is made. A demonstration program:

```
main()
{
char character;
int number;
    character = 'A';
    number = 22;
    number = character;
    character = number;
}
```

The value of the variable `character` remains unchanged because the conversion is reversed. The Atari ST system development version of Alcyon C does not convert characters completely, however.

The conversions shown in this section offer you a great new programming flexibility which BASIC did not offer. All of these possibilities can seem a little confusing at first, but it does not take much practice to become familiar with all of the conversion functions.

5.5 Variable declarations

As we have already made clear, all variables must be declared and thereby given a specific variable type before they are used in a program. The declaration usually takes place in the *header* of a function. But it also may occur anywhere else in the function. The important thing is that the declaration take place before the variable is used.

The declarations in the previous sections and chapters were kept as simple as possible. They generally looked something like this:

```
main()
{
    int a;
    int x;
    long y;
    float b;
    char c;
    ... the rest of the program ...
}
```

Variables can be ordered in any manner inside the declaration. The following declaration sequence is also possible.

```
main()
{
    int a, b, c, d, e;
    int x_value, y_value;
    float symbol_1
          symbol_2;
    ...
}
```

This sequence is shorter and more compact than the previous example.

Until now we have always assigned values to variables at the beginning of the program, right after the declaration section, as in this example:

```
main()
{
    int number;
    number = 123
    ...
}
```

It is also possible to put the declaration and definition together. This has the following syntax:

```
main()
{
     int number = 123;
     ...
}
```

Which version you choose depends upon whether you prefer a compact version like that immediately above, or a more readable version with the value assignment closer to the context of the variable's actual use.

This is all we will say about variable declarations for now. We will look at the declaration of single and multi-dimensional arrays later in the chapter.

5.6 Global/local variables

Until now, we have used only local variables, i.e., variables declared inside a function (usually `main`).

However, C programs usually consist of a set of functions, which are normally called from `main()`.

Here you must decide if you want a variable to be global (applicable to all functions) or if you want it to be local to one function.

Local variables, also called automatic variables, are declared in the function in which they will be used. They are valid only within this function. They are different from variables in BASIC, which are always valid in every function. BASIC has only global variables, which apply to the entire program, including subroutines.

These *global variables* in C are declared before a function, in the same place that symbolic constants are declared.

To make the difference between the two variable types clear, take a look at the following program. The program contains both automatic and global variables, as well as symbolic constants:

```
#define CONSTANT_NUMBER 1234
int glob_int;
char char_global;
main()
{
    char local_char = 'A';
    float float_local;
    /* ... */
}
subroutine(c)
{
    char local_char2;
    /* ... */
}
```

Some important advice: BASIC programmers have a dangerous tendency to declare all variables as global so that they can always use them. This leads to unreadable programs, especially if they have a large number of functions!

5.7 Arrays

You should remember everything you learned in BASIC related to arrays. Virtually all programs use arrays, even if they manage only a tiny amount of data. We have already shown how simple one-dimensional arrays are defined.

The BASIC command:

```
10 DIM A%(10)
```

corresponds to the C statement:

```
int c[10];
```

We declare arrays in the same way we declare all other data types: first the variable type, then the name. All data types in C can be declared as arrays. The size of the array is enclosed in square brackets as a numeric index. After the declaration, you must remember to assign a value to each before using it.

This assignment can be done using a `for` loop, as in this example program:

```
main()
{
    int a[10];
    int i;
    for (i = 0; i <= 10; i = i + 1)
        a[i] = 0;
    ...
}
```

In the initialization condition of the `for` loop, it becomes clear that arrays in C begin with zero rather than one, as in BASIC.

A C array with five elements:

```
int a[5]
```

contains the elements:

```
        a[0]
        a[1]
        a[2]
        a[3]
to      a[4]
```

But the array doesn't contain `a[5]`!

Arrays in C are handled in much the same way as they are in BASIC. For example, if you want to assign the number 12 to the second element of an `a[5]` array (which is `a[1]`), then you simply write:

```
a[1] = 12;
```

Value assignment can be done directly in the initialization, just like the instruction:

```
int c = 12;
```

This has one restriction: it is not possible to initialize local variables.

Global variables are initialized in the declaration as follows:

```
int a[7] = [1, 6, 8, 2, 7, 1, 15];
```

The compiler performs this assignment from left to right. It assigns a value from inside the brackets to each element in the array a.

This instruction can be made even simpler:

```
int a[] = {1, 6, 8, 2, 7, 1, 15};
```

The empty square brackets mean that the size of the array corresponds exactly to the number of assigned elements.

In effect, the compiler counts these elements and places this number inside the brackets.

Once more we would like to stress that this assignment technique does *not* work with local arrays.

Here is an example of the above technique with a global array:

```
int arr[] = {10, 9, 8, 7, 6, 5, 4, 3, 2, 1, 0};
main()
{
    int i;
    for (i = 0; i < 11; ++i)
        printf("%d\n", arr[i]);
}
```

This program assigns the global array `arr` with the values from ten to zero. These values are then printed out in a `for` loop in `main`.

5.7.1 Multi-dimensional arrays

In BASIC we declare a five-by-five array as follows:

```
10 DIM A%(5,5)
```

In C, the same assignment looks like this:

```
int a[5][5];
```

If we want to address a specific element of the array, it is done as follows:

```
a[2][4] = 12;
```

Don't forget that again you must assign a value to each element before use. With local variables, the best way to do this is with a `for` loop. With global or static variables, the following initialization technique will declare the array and fill it with numbers simultaneously:

```
static int field[3][5] = {{1, 2, 3, 4, 5},
                         {2, 3, 4, 5, 6},
                         {4, 5, 6, 7, 8}};
```

5.7.2 Strings

For the sake of thoroughness we would like to mention some facts once again about strings. Precisely defined, strings are nothing more than one-dimensional arrays of characters. All information necessary for you to use strings has already been covered.

A string is an array of characters terminated by the null character \0. The *string:*

```
"A"
```

is not the same as the *character:*

```
'A'
```

This is because the string contains the null character in addition to the letter A, to mark the end of the string. Thus the string consists of two characters: the 'A' and the '\0'. The character consists only of the 'A'.

A string can also be declared globally as a character array. This is done in a program as follows:

```
char string_char[] = "I am a string";
    main()
    {
        printf("%s\n", string_char);
        gemdos(0x1);
    }
```

But this is possible only with global or static variables. The string instruction %s in printf causes the global string to be printed.

We solved the problem of assignment to local variables with the pointer marker *. In a program, it looked something like this:

```
    main()
    {
        char *string_char;
        string_char = "I am a string";
            printf("%s\n", string_char);
        gemdos(0x1);
    }
```

The next chapter contains a detailed explanation of how this works and why it must be done this way.

Chapter 6

C Pointers

C Pointers

Pointers and arrays are very closely related in C. All operations we've carried out so far with arrays can also be done with pointers. Before we go into exactly what this relation is, it would be a good idea to find out what pointers really are—and what they can do.

6.1 Pointer fundamentals

Unless you have written routines in machine code, or your BASIC supported VARPTR, you have probably never used pointers. Even with the VARPTR command, BASIC is not well set up to make use of pointers.

But pointers are one of the primary features of C. You can't really tap the potential of C without first mastering pointers.

What is a pointer, anyway? A *pointer* is a variable that holds the address of another variable. This definition sounds a bit complicated, but the following example should make it more clear.

When a variable name is defined, it is nothing but a placeholder for a value. Variable names are then used instead of memory addresses in the computer. An assignment like this:

```
int value1 = 15;
```

causes the value 15 to be copied into the memory location allocated to `value1`.

Pointers let you work directly with memory addresses. It looks like this in a program:

```
addr_value1 = &value1
```

The & character, called the *address operator*, tells the compiler that the variable `addr_value1` is to be assigned the value of the address of the variable `value1`—i.e. `addr_value1` is the pointer to `value1`.

To explain this we should first look at another pointer operator, *. We have already seen this character in conjunction with strings, but it has not been explained yet.

The * character preceding a pointer returns the <u>value</u> that the pointer points to, instead of the value of the pointer itself (an address). This may seem somewhat complicated, but it is really quite simple.

Assume that `addr_value1` is a pointer to the variable `value1`. With the assignment:

```
value2 = *addr_value1;
```

the variable `value2` is assigned the contents of the address to which `addr_value1` points.

For example, if the value assigned to `value1` is 15, then the pointer `addr_value1` contains the address of where this value is stored in the ST.

With the assignment:

```
value2 = *addr_value1;
```

`value2` receives the value 15, which is stored at the address to which `addr_value1` points. The contents of `value2` therefore correspond to the original value of `value1`, which is 15.

Written in one segment, our example program looks like this:

```
main()
{
    int value1, value2, *addr_value1;
    value1 = 15;
    addr_value1 = &value1;
    value2 = *addr_value1;
}
```

The preceding program has the same result as the following program, which does not use a pointer:

```
main()
{
    int value1, value2;
    value1 = 15;
    value2 = value1;
}
```

The two assignments:

```
addr_value1 = &value1;
value2 = *addr_value1;
```

are equivalent to the simple assignment:

```
value2 = value1;
```

Note: the prerelease version of Alcyon C does not handle the assignment of pointer addresses and pointer contents correctly. The statement:

```
&value2 = *addr_value1;
```

is not executed completely. All other ST compilers available on the market adhere to the standard.

In summary:

Pointers are introduced by placing the address operator (&) in front of a variable. This expression then returns the address of the contents of the variable in memory:

```
addr_value1 = &value1;
```

In this expression, the pointer `addr_value1` is assigned the address of the variable `value1`.

The contents of the memory address to which a pointer points can be obtained using the * operator.

6.2 Using pointers

Now that you know what pointers are and what they do, you need to know the best ways to use them in programs. At times you'll find that pointers are the only way to perform certain calculations. You will probably not run into cases like these when you are first learning C, however.

Pointers are among the major strengths of C and are generally necessary for tight, elegant programs. At the same time, pointers must be used with extreme care.

Improper use of pointers can hopelessly mangle a program, and break all the rules for optimal, well-structured programming. The reason for this is largely because it is easy to insert a pointer that points just "anywhere."

One important use of pointers lies in the manipulation of data between individual functions. We will cover this in detail in the chapter on functions. Another major use of pointers is the management of arrays. We'll explain this next.

6.3 Pointers and arrays

As we said at the beginning of this chapter, pointers and arrays are very closely related. We have demonstrated this through the use of strings. String variables must be used as pointers of the form:

```
char *string;
string = "Hello, how are you?";
```

We will explain this and many other details about arrays and pointers on the following pages.

6.4 Numeric arrays

Let's define a one-dimensional array with 15 elements:

```
float x[15];
```

We thus obtain an array with the elements x[0] through x[14].

Now let's declare a pointer call (pointer) to a float value:

```
float *pointer;
```

The instruction:

```
pointer = &x[0];
```

assigns the address of the first element of array x to pointer.

As we have already found out, we can find the contents of the address to which a pointer points with the following command:

```
value = *pointer
```

This assigns the value of x[0] to the variable value.

If *pointer contains the value of the first element of the x array (x[0]), then we can define the value:

```
*(pointer + 1)
```

This is the next element of the array. *(pointer + 1) corresponds to the value of x[1].

In general terms, *(pointer + i) is identical to x[i], provided that pointer points to the start of x as it does in our example.

Now let's go a bit further. The expression which we used earlier:

```
pointer = &x[0];
```

can also be written as follows:

```
pointer = x;
```

The address of the first element of an array thus has the same value as the name of the array. Why?

During compilation, an array reference is automatically converted to the address of the first element plus an offset to the element being accessed. Because the name of an array is thus identified with the address of its first element, the assignment `pointer = x` is allowed.

This means that the expression:

```
x[i]
```

is converted to the form:

```
*(x + i);
```

The two expressions for the ith element of the x array are completely equivalent and interchangable. This means that:

> x[i]   and   (x + i)

are completely equivalent.

This equivalence also applies to the use of the address operator (&):

> (x + i)   and   &x[i]

are completely identical.

In other words, x + i represents the address of the ith element of the array x.

This is also true for the pointer. It can be used with the square brackets and an array index as a replacement for the original array variable (provided the two are equal):

    `pointer[i]`   is the same as   `*(pointer + i)`

It then follows that any pointer that points to an array can be used in exactly the same way as the array name itself, and with the same results. It is therefore logical that every array element has its own pointer.

All of these pointers correspond to the ascending order of the individual array elements and are assigned in a uniform, ascending order. The first pointer points to the first element of the array, the second pointer points the second element, and so on.

All of these pointers can be used either in the form:

    `pointer[i]`

or in the form:

    `*(pointer + i)`

All of these explanations were demonstrated with examples using one-dimensional arrays, but everything said here applies without exception to multi-dimensional arrays as well.

Make sure that you really understand all of the details in this section. If not, then carefully go through the section again. You should also try out the examples in some programs of your own.

You will need this information when we leave numeric arrays and look at character arrays again. Everything we have said about numeric arrays and pointers applies to all other data types, including characters.

Character arrays, or strings, still have a few differences, which we will explain next.

6.5 Strings and arrays

A string is nothing more than a one-dimensional array of characters. The string

```
"C is the programming language of the future!"
```

is represented in the computer as an array.

The compiler terminates the array with a null character ('\0'). C has no special functions for managing strings as such, because strings are simply treated as character arrays.

Until now we have created strings as in this example:

```
main()
{
    char *string;
    string = "ATARI ST";
    printf("%s\n", string);
    gemdos(0x1);
}
```

The expression:

```
char *string;
```

is the same as:

```
char string[];
```

In this example it becomes clear that the strings in our previous programs were one-dimensional arrays.

The statements:

```
char *string;
```

and:

```
char string[];
```

set up an array of undetermined length. This array will later be filled with elements. This is done as follows:

```
string = "any text ...";
```

Here, the variable `string` is simply assigned a pointer to the characters in the string. The string itself is not copied—the pointer is simply assigned the address of the string.

With the assignment:

```
string = "any text ...";
```

the variable `string` points to the first element of the array, in this case the a in any.

At first this may seem strange to BASIC programmers. For now, we will consider it enough to know what pointers are and how they are used. But rest assured that you will encounter pointers again and again in this book.

Pointers are also important for working with functions. You will learn more about this in the chapter specifically devoted to functions in C.

Chapter 7

Arithmetic Operators and Expressions

Arithmetic Operators and Expressions

If you worked through the previous chapter thoroughly, you should be able to go through this chapter with somewhat less trouble. The elementary arithmetic operations are practically the same as those you know from BASIC. C, however, has a whole set of operators which we must go through in detail yet. C possesses some very powerful arithmetic functions which are not found in BASIC at all. We covered a few of these special functions and differences from BASIC briefly in the introductory chapter.

On the following pages, we will explain these and other new arithmetic properties of C, in detailed comparison to BASIC.

7.1 What are operators?

In the BASIC expression

```
10 PRINT 1+5/7
```

the symbols + and / are the operators. They work with the constants 1, 5, and 7. Operators are used in C the same way they are used in BASIC.

Look over the following list comparing BASIC and C arithmetic commands:

	BASIC instruction	C instruction
1.	PRINT 1+5/7	printf("%f\n", 1 + 5 / 7);
2.	PRINT 2.2+(4*2)/7	printf("%f\n", 2.2 + (4.0 * 2.0) / 7.0);
3.	A=888*3	a = 888 * 3;
4.	A=5-6*2+(3*3)/2	a = 5 - 6 * 2 + (3 * 3) / 2;
5.	A=A+1	a = a + 1; or also ++a;

7.2 Value assignments

Now that you have seen some of the similarities between the arithmetic operations of BASIC and C, let's look at some of the differences.

The BASIC expression

```
10 A=A+1
```

can be written the same way in C:

```
a = a + 1;
```

Another form is possible in C:

```
a += 1;
```

This version is much more compact in long expressions. In a = a + 1; the name a is repeated on the left and right sides of the equals sign. There is no repetition when the combined operator in a += 1; is used.

This operator combination is possible with all of the operators we have seen so far:

```
    +     -     *     /
```

and also with the following new C operators, which we will explore in detail later in this chapter:

```
    %    >>    <<    &    ^    |
```

The arithmetic expression

```
value_1 = value_1 * 20;
```

can be written more compactly as follows:

```
value_1 *= 20;
```

In general, if EXP1 and EXP2 are expressions, then it is true that

```
           EXP1 operand= EXP2;
example:   a        +  =   1 ;
```

is completely equivalent to

```
           EXP1 = (EXP1) operand (EXP2);
example:   a    =   a       +      1   ;
```

Note the parentheses around EXP1 and EXP2 in the above expression. These are set internally by the computer and ensure that:

```
z /= x + 2;
```

really corresponds to:

```
z = z / (x + 2);
```

and not :

```
z = z / x + 2;
```

where z is divided by x and the result divided by 2, rather than the intended result of z being divided by (x + 2).

You will soon come to like this capability which C offers you. It lets you write expressions more compactly and efficiently.

An example—assume that you want to make the assignment:

```
arrwt_1e2[zz[aa]] = arrwt_1e2[zz[aa]] * 22;
```

Using the new assignment operator, you can write it better as:

```
arrwt_1e2[zz[aa]] *= 22;
```

One advantage of this capability is that you can avoid many unnecessary errors by not having to repeat a complex variable on both sides of the equal sign.

Also, assignments are much easier to understand, especially for other users of your program. You don't have to spend a lot of time making sure that the expression on the right of the equals sign is identical to the expression on the left.

Furthermore, this formulation saves memory space in compilation and allows more efficient machine code to be generated.

7.3 The modulo operator

This operator is not available in many versions of BASIC, though it is available in ST BASIC as MOD. It returns the remainder of an integer division.

In C this can be done using the following expression:

```
remainder = a % b;
```

The variable `remainder` is assigned the remainder of the division of a by b.

There is, however, one limitation to the use of modulo operator. The modulo operator cannot be used for `double` or `float` values, but only for integers (`int`) and characters (`char`).

7.4 The increment and decrement operators

Now that you have learned that the expression:

```
x = x + 1;
```

which looks fairly familiar to BASIC programmers, can also be written more compactly as:

```
x += 1;
```

We will cover another, even more compact formulation using the increment operator.

This operator looks very unusual to a BASIC programmer and reads:

```
++x;
```

We also have the corresponding decrement operator, --. An example of its use is the following expression:

```
--x;
```

This is the same as:

```
x = x - 1;
```

The decrement operator -- is the opposite of the increment operator ++ and reduces the value of its operand by one. The increment operator, on the other hand, increases the value of its operand by one.

The increment and decrement operators are rather unusual in that they can be used both before and after the operand. Both the prefix notation:

```
--x;
```

and the postfix notation:

```
x--;
```

are possible.

At first glance there is no practical difference between the two versions. In both cases, the value of the variable is reduced by one. The difference comes into play when the operators are used within other expressions since these operators return a value just like all operators in C.

In these cases, --x causes x to be decremented before the variable is used so that the value of the expression --x is the original value of x minus 1. x--, on the other hand, causes x to be decremented after it is used and the value of x-- is equal simply to the original value of x.

This may sound a little dry but it can be easily demonstrated with an example:

Assume that the variable x has the value 2. In the assignment:

```
y = ++x;
```

the incrementation takes place before the expression is evaluated and the variable y is assigned the value of 2 + 1, or 3. The variable x also now has the value of 3.

However, in the assignment:

```
y = x++;
```

the variable y is assigned the value 2. After the assignment the value of x is incremented to 3.

For further clarification, let's look at the BASIC versions of these two notations:

```
y = x++; corresponds to 10 Y=X
                       20 X=X+1
```

and

```
y = ++x; corresponds to 10 X=X+1
                       20 Y=X
```

The availability of the increment and decrement operators opens up many elegant programming possibilities. You will find these operators used in almost every C program.

7.5 Comparison operators

In BASIC we have the following comparison operators available to us:

```
<     ........ less than
>     ........ greater than
<=    ........ less than or equal to
>=    ........ greater than or equal to
```

All of these BASIC operators are exactly the same in C. Here you should not have any problems changing over to C.

Now we come to the equivalence operators. In BASIC these are

```
=     ........ equal to
```

and

```
<>    ........ not equal to
```

These are different from those in C. In C, they are

```
==    ........ equal to
```

and

```
!=    ........ not equal to
```

In spite of these formal differences, the use of equivalence operators in C is identical to that in BASIC. You need only remember the new symbols == and !=.

It will be easy for you with your BASIC experience to confuse the assignment operator, =, and the equivalence operator, ==.

Now we'll briefly show you the most important uses of the comparison and equivalence operators. For the most part, they are used with control structures. We'll explain these in the next chapter. The most common control structure is the `if` statement.

As in this BASIC program:

```
10 A=2
20 IF A=2 THEN PRINT "OK!"
```

In C, the above becomes

```
main()
{
    int a = 2;
    if(a == 2)
        {
            printf("OK!\n");
        }
    gemdos(0x1);
}
```

Another area of use is in `while` loops. The `while` statement can be implemented as follows:

```
#include "stdio.h"
main()
{
    int a = 12;
    while(a <= 11)
        {
            puts("All clear!");
        }
    gemdos(0x1);
}
```

Even more common is the use of comparison and equivalence operators in `for` loops. Here is a short program to demonstrate:

```
main()
{
    int x;
    for(x = 0; x <= 20; ++x);
        printf("%d\n", x);
    gemdos(0x1);
}
```

The loop counts from zero through twenty, using the comparison operator "less than or equal to", <=.

The four comparison operations:

```
<
<=
>=
>
```

all have the same execution priority. Comparing them to the equivalence operators == and !=, we find that the comparison operators have the higher priority, while the equivalence operators share the same priority.

7.6 Logical combinations

The logical operations in BASIC are AND and OR. Their meanings are self-explanatory. The corresponding C operators are less obvious to the BASIC programmer.

They are:

```
&&   ......... and
```

and

```
||   ......... or
```

In spite of the different forms of the C expressions, they are used in exactly the same way.

The BASIC line:

```
10 IF A=1 AND B=2 OR B=1 THEN PRINT "Condition met!"
```

is translated to C as:

```
main()
{
    int a = 1;
    int b = 2;
    if (a == 1 && b == 2 || b == 1)
        printf("Condition met!\n");
    gemdos(0x1);
}
```

As you can see, the makeup of the expressions is identical. You should have no difficulty adapting from BASIC here.

7.7 The negation operator

This operator is similar to the BASIC bit operator NOT. C has two different negation operators. The first is the logical negation operator ! The second is the bitwise negation operator ~. When dealing with a logical expression, such as one involving a comparison, the logical operator ! should be used. It changes a zero value to a one and a non-zero value to a zero. There is no direct BASIC counterpart to the logical negation operator in C.

Note the C program below:

```
main()
{
    int value = 0;
    if(value == 0)
        printf("ZERO!!!\n");
    gemdos(0x1);
}
```

This program can also be formulated as follows:

```
main()
{
    int value = 0;
    if(!value)
        printf("ZERO!!!\n");
    gemdos(0x1);
}
```

You might ask how the the expression:

```
if(value == 0)
```

can be replaced simply with:

```
if(!value)
```

The exclamation point in front of the variable `value` is the negation operator. This operator is always used as a prefix before the operand.

This produces a logical 1 when a variable which it preceeds is equal to zero. The compiler interprets all logical values not equal to zero as "true." A zero is always viewed as "false." So if the contents of the variable `value` are not equal to zero, the negation operator returns a logical zero, or false.

If this were the case, the command following the `if` condition would not be executed. You could quickly demonstrate this by changing the assignment statement in our example program to:

```
int value = 2;
```

Once again, the expression:

```
if (value == 0)
```

is identical to the shorter form using the negation operator:

```
if (!value)
```

The logical negation operator can also be used in conjunction with the other logical operators to produce NAND, NOR, and other functions.

7.8 Multiple assignments

Unlike BASIC, C allows multiple assignments. For example, an expression like:

```
a = b = c = d = 15;
```

is allowed and is functionally equivalent to the following series of assignments:

```
a = 15;
b = 15;
c = 15;
d = 15;
```

or alternatively:

```
d = 15;
c = d;
b = c;
a = b;
```

All of the variables are assigned the same value by this combined assignment statement.

Variables can also be assigned in addition to constants like the 15 used in our example. An example of this is the instruction:

```
value_1 = value_2 = value_3 = variable5;
```

This line assigns the contents of variables to the variables `value_1` through `value_3`.

Multiple assignments allow a more compact and effective programming style which takes up less memory space.

We have now covered all of the important arithmetic operators. Now let's look at the bit operators in the next section.

7.9 The bit operators

Because C is a system language, it offers a whole series of special operations for the manipulation of bits. These are assembled in the following list:

Bit operator   Function

```
|         "or" operation on bits
&         "and" operation on bits
<<        shift bits left
>>        shift bits right
^         "exclusive or" operation bits
~         one's complement or bit inversion
```

All of these *bit operators* are used in the same manner as the normal ones which we have already explained in the sections on arithmetic. They may not, however, be used with `float` or `double` variables.

A chart follows, showing a few ways in which these operators can be used in arithmetic expressions:

Example of use: Function accomplished:

```
x = y & 011       Sets bits to zero.
y = y | mask;     Sets bits to one.
y << 4            Shifts y four bits to the left.
y >> 2            Shifts y two bits to the right.
y & 077           Masks out bits in an integer value.
```

We will now leave our brief introduction to bit operators and their applications. This book was conceived for BASIC programmers and other newcomers to C. Manipulation of bits is a theme you will not need until you want to try your hand at advanced systems programming. A comprehensive overview of this specialized aspect of C would really accomplish nothing other than to scare the average BASIC programmer.

If, however, you have some machine language programming experience, you should now be able to use these bit operators in your programs with the help of this short introduction.

You can also try out a few of these operations on your own, even if you are a beginner. But in practice you'll find you need these operations only for specialized systems programming for which detailed system knowledge is also necessary.

In summary, we can state that any bit operation which is carried out in BASIC with the AND and OR operators is carried out using the bitwise operators found on the previous pages.

The BASIC bit operation:

```
10 X = 7 AND 1
```

is written in C as:

```
x = 7 & 1;
```

Chapter 8

Control Structures in C

Control Structures in C

Control structures are the core of every programming language. They make it possible to specify which operations the computer should execute at a given time. In essence, they are used to determine the order in which actions are carried out.

8.1 Control structures in BASIC

The following control structures are available in most common varieties of BASIC:

```
IF  ... THEN
FOR ... NEXT
ON  ... GOTO
```

Some more structured BASIC dialects also offer statements like

```
IF ... THEN ... ELSE
```

and

```
WHILE ... WEND
```

All of these BASIC structures are found in C, although some of the syntax is a little different. In addition, you have a whole series of powerful possibilities for the control of program execution which are not available in BASIC.

8.2 The `if` statement

We have already used the if statement in the previous chapters. For example, we determined that the program:

```
10 X=15
20 Y=X
30 IF X=Y THEN [Execute the following commands]
```

is formulated in C as:

```
main()
{
    int x, y;
    x = 15;
    y = x;
    if(x == y)
        {
            then execute the commands
            here inside the brackets;
        }
}
```

The syntax for the IF command in BASIC:

```
IF [expression] THEN [execute commands]
```

is expressed as follows in C:

```
if(expression)
    [execute commands;]
```

As this statement is executed, the computer checks if the arithmetic expression in the parentheses is true or false. As we have already observed, C considers a logical zero to be false and any other logical value to be true.

If the expression is true, then the statement following the expression is executed. Note that multiple statements can be combined into a block as a single statement with the curly braces {}.

We can shorten our statements with this background knowledge about the logic of evaluation in the `if` statement. We already covered one of these abbreviations, which used the negation operator (!) in the chapter on aritthmetic.

Let's review:

```
if(value == 0)
```

can be written with the use of the negation operator in a more compact form as:

```
if(!value)
```

Another clear simplification involves the use of:

```
if(value)
```

instead of:

```
if(value != 0)
```

If this variable `value` does not equal zero, the condition is viewed to be true, without having to use the !=0 test, and the statements following the `if` statement are executed.

Here is a summary of the information about the `if` statement from the previous chapters:

Any of the comparison and equivalence operators can be used in the condition of an `if` statement:

```
<
>
<=
>=
==
```

as well as:

```
!=
```

Comparison operators of the form:

>   =<

and:

>   =>

are not allowed.

AND instructions, as has been already explained, are represented by:

>   &&

and the OR instruction by:

> ||

An example: The BASIC line:

```
10 IF A=4 OR X>=3 AND B<>6 THEN [execute]
```

is translated in C to:

```
if(a == 4 || x >= 3 && b != 6)
   {
        execute;
   }
```

Watch out for the following error in your C programs:

```
if(a = 4 || x >= 3 && b != 6)
   (...)
```

Here the assignment operator = is confused with the comparison operator ==. This mistake is very typical for programmers who are used to BASIC.

As the assignment and equality operators in BASIC use the same character, you must pay close attention when translating an algorithm to C.

If we translate the following program into C:

```
10 INPUT Y%
20 IF Y%=15 THEN PRINT "THIS IS THE ANSWER":
                PRINT "THE NUMBER 15 IS CORRECT!"
```

we get:

```
main()
{
    int y;
    scanf("%d", &y);
    if (y == 15)
        {
            printf("This is the answer\n");
            printf("The number 15 is correct!\n");
        }
    gemdos(0x1);
}
```

With this example you see once again that if more than one statement is to be executed, they must all be enclosed in curly braces. The braces may be left off if only one statement follows the `if` statement.

It is also possible to combine several `if` statements. Such a combination, which corresponds to the AND operation, is demonstrated in the following C program fragment:

```
if(a != 4)
  if (b == 12)
    if (x > 5)
      printf("All conditions fulfilled!");
```

This is the same as the following expression using logical AND:

```
if(a != 4 && b == 12 && x > 5)
   printf("All conditions fulfilled!");
```

8.2.1 The `exit()` statement

Let's say that you want to adapt our previous BASIC example to C:

```
10 INPUT Y%
20 IF Y%=15 THEN PRINT "THAT'S THE ANSWER!"
30 END
```

The main difference is END (line 30). Now for the C translation:

```c
main()
{
    int y;
    scanf("%d", &y);
    if (y == 15)
      printf("That's the answer!\n");
    exit(0);
}
```

You are already familiar with the program from the previous pages and it needs no further explanation. It is almost an exact duplicate of the previous C program.

Until now, however, we have not seen the function `exit()`, which is called in the statement:

```c
exit(0);
```

The argument we use is not important for this application. The argument, in this case zero (0), is passed backed to the function which called `exit()`. In our example this is passed back to `main()`.

In this C program, the call to `exit()` is comparable to the END command in BASIC. The statement is quite useful in a program like the following:

```
10 INPUT Y$
20 IF Y$="STOP" THEN END
25 REM
30 PRINT "LET'S KEEP GOING..."
```

This is translated into C as follows:

```
main()
{
    char *y;
    scanf("%s", y);
    if (y == "stop")
       exit(0);
    printf("Continuing...\n");
    gemdos(0x1);
}
```

The `exit(0)` call is quite important in this program. It ends the program just like BASIC `END` instruction and ensures that the `printf` command which prints "Continuing..." is not executed if you've told the program to stop.

In the first C program in this section, the `exit()` statement was not needed. The program would have ended automatically because there were no additional commands. In the program above, however, we needed it to accomplish our purpose. This exit command is very useful in conjunction with `goto` statements. More about this later in the chapter.

The Alcyon C for the Atari ST also offers another similar function. Its syntax is

```
abort(0);
```

This function exits the current program and generates an error.

8.2.2 The if-else test

Every normal `if` statement test can also have a `else` part added. Some versions of BASIC allow the following program which contains an `ELSE` statement.

```
10 INPUT A%
20 IF A%<20 THEN PRINT A%*A% ELSE PRINT "THE NORMAL
        VALUE IS:";A%
```

This is also possible in C:

```
main()
{
    int a;
    scanf("%d", &a);
    if (a < 20)
        printf("%d\n", a * a);
    else
        {
            printf("The normal value is: ");
            printf("%d\n", a);
        }
    gemdos(0x1);
}
```

The `else` portion corresponds to the syntax of the `if` statement in that no semicolon follows it, and that if you want more than one statement to follow it they must be enclosed in curly braces, as in our example.

In general, the `if-else` construction in C is represented as follows:

```
if (condition fulfilled)
   {
     execute command block  1
   }

else
   {
     execute command block  2
   }
```

8.2.3 Combining `if-else` statements

This construction can be expanded with any number of `if` and `else` statements. This leads to a problem.

Let's say you find the following section in a program.

```
if(a == 2)
if(b != 15)
   a = a * 2;
else
   a = a * 3;
```

Here we have to figure out which `if` statement the `else` statement belongs to, the first or the second. An `else` statement always applies to the `if` immediately preceeding it. So in this case the `else` statement belongs to the second `if` statement, `if(b != 15)`.

If the `else` is supposed to belong to the first `if`, you have to indicate this by adding braces. In our example, this change would look like this:

Old version:	New version:

```if(a == 2)```
   ```if(b != 15)```
      ```a = a * 2;```
```else```
   ```a = a * 3;```
	```if(a == 2)```
	  ```{```
	   ```if(b != 15)```
	      ```a = a * 2;```
	  ```}```
	```else```
	   ```a = a * 3;```

8.2.4 `else-if` chains

Combinations of `if` and `else` statements are often used. The `else-if` construction looks like this:

```
if(condition 1 fulfilled)
   execute command block 1
      else if(condition 2 fulfilled)
         execute command block 2
      ...
         else if(condition n-1 fulfilled)
            execute command block n-1
               else
                  execute command block n
```

The advantage of this method is that it allows one of a variety alternatives to be selected.

The conditions are evaluated in order and when one is met the corresponding block of commands is executed and the search through the `else-if` chain is terminated.

The last statement,

```
else
    execute command block n
```

is not always necessary.

The last statement is often used because it handles the situation when none of the conditions are fulfilled. It can recognize errors or illegal input and take care of the trouble before it can cause problems later in the program.

We will now leave our detailed explanation of `if` and `else` statements and their combinations to discuss another control structure, the `for` loop. After that we will cover the `while` loop and the special `do-while` construction.

8.3 `for` loops

We have already used this loop in a number of examples in our introductory chapter. First, we will quickly review what we already learned and then we will discuss additional details about `for` loops in C.

8.3.1 Review and summary

As we determined, the C statement

```
for(x = 1; x <= 20; x = x + 2)
    {
        loop contents to be repeated
    }
```

is identical to the familiar BASIC FOR-NEXT loop

```
FOR X=1 TO 20 STEP +2
    loop contents to be repeated
NEXT X
```

The loop declaration

```
for(x = 1; x <= 20; x = x + 2)
```

in C is divided into three parts, just as it is in BASIC.

The first part in our example, `x = 1;`, determines the initial value of the loop. This part could be translated to English as "Start the loop with the x-value of 1." This part corresponds to the BASIC `FOR X=1`. After that comes `x <= 20`, comparable with `TO 20` in BASIC, which defines the end of the interval during which the loop is repeated. The third part, `x = x + 2`, determines the step size and is roughly equivalent to the BASIC `STEP +2`.

The step size must always be specified explicitly in C. This includes an increment of +1, which can be omitted in BASIC, but is written in C as

```
x = x + 1
```

or more compactly as

```
++x;
```

The statement immediately following the `for` loop in C is always repeated. If more than one statement is to be executed inside the `for` loop they must be combined into a statement block within curly braces.

8.3.2 Infinite loops

If you leave the three parts—the initial value, the end value, and the increment size—out of a `for` loop, the result is an infinite loop and it looks like this:

```
for(;;)
    {
            commands to be repeated endlessly
    }
```

The reason for the infinite repetition of the commands is that the compiler interperets the middle parameter (the end interval of the loop) as the test of a condition. In other words, the result is checked only to see if it is true or false. It makes no difference to the compiler what condition is used for the middle parameter.

Because an empty middle parameter is not equal to a binary zero, it is viewed as true and the compiler never exits the loop. With the following program, for example, the letter "H" is printed on the screen in a continuous loop:

```
main()
{
    for(;;)
        printf("%c", 'H');
}
```

It is also possible to write infinite loops in BASIC, such as with the instruction:

```
FOR X=Y TO Z STEP 0
```

The STEP 0 causes the loop to be repeated indefinitely. Our example C program would look like this in BASIC:

```
10 FOR X=1 TO 2 STEP 0
20 PRINT "H";
30 NEXT X
```

Here, however, you must make sure that there is a difference between the lower and upper bounds.

```
10 FOR X=1 TO 1 STEP 0
```

does not cause an endless loop, but these will:

```
10 FOR X=1 TO 4 STEP 0
```

```
10 FOR X=1 TO -30 STEP 0
```

Infinite loops in C can only be terminated by break or goto statements. We will see how to use these in the following sections of this chapter.

Since only the middle statement of the loop declaration matters here, the following program also causes an infinite loop.

```
#include "stdio.h"
#define putchar(c) putc(c,stdout)
main()
{
    char y;
    for(y = 'H';;)
        putchar(y);
}
```

This example also prints the letter H on the screen repeatedly, but the variable is assigned right in the for loop this time. The middle parameter is still empty, however, so the compiler still considers it to be true.

For this reason, the following program does not result in an infinite loop:

```
main()
{
    int a;
    for (a = 1; a < 20; )
        {
            printf("%d\n", a * a);
            a++;
        }
    gemdos(0x1);
}
```

It is not the same as the BASIC program:

```
10 FOR A=1 TO 20
20 PRINT A*A
30 NEXT A
```

but much more like the following version in which the incrementation also takes place within the loop:

```
10 FOR A=1 TO 20 STEP 0
20 PRINT A*A;
30 A=A+1
40 NEXT A
```

Infinite loops are not often used in BASIC programs (not on purpose, anyway), but they more common in C because of the availability of the `goto` and `break` statements.

8.3.3 The comma operator

This special C operator is most often used in conjunction with the `for` statement, but it can be used in other applications as well. Two expressions separated by a comma are evaluated from left to right. This means that the data type and value of the result of one statement are automatically the data type and value of the operand to the right of the comma.

This allows multiple statements to be combined. First, the statement to the left of the comma operator is executed, and then the one on the right is performed.

The following program illustrates the comma operator in a `for` loop.

```
main()
{
    int a, c;
    for (a = 1, c = 15; c < 30; a--, c++)
        printf("%d n%d\n", a, c);
    gemdos(0x1);
}
```

As you can see in this example, the flexibility of the `for` loop can be greatly increased using the comma operator. It can be used in both the initialization and in the incrementation sections of the loop declaration.

The loop declaration:

```
for(a = 1, c = 15; c < 30; a--, c++)
```

includes two simultaneous initializations:

```
a = 1, c = 15;
```

The same is true for the incrementation part of the loop:

```
a--, c++
```

The increment and decrement instructions joined together by the comma are executed at the same time.

8.3.4 Nested for loops

Just as in BASIC, C for loops can be nested within each other. A BASIC example is the program:

```
10 FOR A%=1 TO 50
20 FOR B%=20 TO 1 STEP -1
30 PRINT A%, B%
40 NEXT B%
50 NEXT A%
```

The following program shows how this loop construction would be accomplished in C. This has exactly the same results as the BASIC program above.

```
main()
    {
        int a, b;
        for (a = 1; a <= 50; ++a)
            for(b = 20; b >= 1; --b)
                printf("%d %d\n", a, b);
        gemdos(0x1);
    }
```

The curly braces can be omitted here because the for loop consists of just one line.

Now let's add two lines to our previous BASIC program:

```
10 FOR A%=1 TO 50
20 FOR B%=20 TO 1 STEP -1
30 PRINT A%, B%
40 PRINT "X^2 VALUE     Y^2 VALUE"
50 PRINT A%*A%, B%*B%
60 NEXT B%
70 NEXT A%
```

In C, the two new PRINT instructions are simply added to the second loop by making a statement block containing them and the original printf call.

For clarification, here is the modified program:

```c
main()
{
  int a, b;
  for (a = 1; a <= 50; ++a)
    for(b = 20; b >= 1; --b)
    {
      printf("%d %d\n", a, b);
      printf("x^2 value    y^2 value\n");
      printf("%d    %d\n", a * a, b * b);
    }
  gemdos(0x1);
}
```

You must also use these brackets if you want to call additional functions between the loops. A corresponding example of our previous BASIC program reads:

```
10 FOR A%=1 TO 50
20 FOR B%=20 TO 1 STEP -1
30 PRINT A%, B%
40 PRINT "X^2 VALUE     Y^2 VALUE"
50 PRINT A%*A%, B%*B%
60 NEXT B%
70 PRINT "OUTER LOOP"
80 NEXT A%
```

In translating this program to C you must use brackets to build statement blocks as follows:

```
main()
{
    int a, b;
    for (a = 1; a <= 50; ++a)
    {
        for(b = 20; b >= 1; --b)
        {
            printf("%d %d\n", a, b);
            printf("x^2 value    y^2 value\n");
            printf("%d    %d\n", a * a, b * b);
        }
        printf("Outer loop\n");
    }
    gemdos(0x1);
}
```

Look at the command structure carefully. First an inner loop is formed as a statement block. The block:

```
{
    printf("%d %d\n", a, b);
    printf("x^2 value    y^2 value\n");
    printf("%d %d\n", a * a, b * b);
}
```

is repeated twenty times via the second `for` statement, until the variable b is equal to one. The outer loop is then executed.

Next there is the command:

```
printf("Outer loop\n");
```

which prints an appropriate message. This happens 50 times as determined by the variable a. This variable is incremented by one up to fifty by the first `for` declaration.

As we know, it is generally shorter and more efficient to declare a step size using the increment operator, as in the example above.

```
++x;
```

should be used instead of the old form:

```
x = x + 1;
```

with which we are familiar from BASIC.

The same goes for the decrement operator:

```
--x;
```

which should generally be used instead of:

```
x = x - 1;
```

Of course this applies only to increment/decrement values of one. The expression for an increment size of +2, for example, must be written like this:

```
x = x + 2;
```

or like this:

```
x += 2;
```

8.4 `while` loops

Now that we have covered the more common `for` loops, its time to turn to a discussion of `while` loops. In the following examples, it must be noted that not all versions of BASIC support `while` loops. The ST BASIC does support them and the construction used is standard in Microsoft BASIC, so we will include examples of `while` loops in BASIC.

Don't worry if you've never used `while` loops before. The syntax is easy to understand and it is also easy to see where you might want to use them. Let's take the following Microsoft BASIC program as an example:

```
10 REM COUNT FROM 1 TO 10
20 '
30 WHILE A%<10
40 A%=A%+1
50 PRINT A%
60 WEND
```

As you can see, the WHILE construction forms a block beginning with the WHILE statement itself and ending with WEND, which is short for "WHILE END".

The commands inside this block are repeated for as long as the WHILE condition, in our case,

```
A%<10
```

is true. The command can be read "While the value of the variable A is less than 10, do the following." The variable A, initialized to zero by the RUN command, is incremented from 1 to 10, and each value is printed on the screen.

How does this look in C? This is the program corresponding to our BASIC example:

```
main()
{
    int a;
    a = 0;
    while (a < 10)
    {
        ++a;
        printf("%d\n", a);
    }
    gemdos(0x1);
}
```

The syntax of the `while` statement in C is almost exactly the same as that of the BASIC `WHILE` command:

```
while (a < 10)
```

Again, the statements in the command block are executed "so long as the value of the variable a is less than 10." But make sure that the variables used in the loop are declared and given values before the actual `while` statement. This is not necessary in BASIC because the variable a is automatically set to zero by the `RUN` command.

In C, however, both the declaration:

```
int a;
```

and the value assignment:

```
a = 0;
```

are necessary. They can both be done in one statement, as we have mentioned before, like this:

```
int a = 0;
```

Note also that the incrementation, which in our example is ++a, must always be specified explicitly within the loop.

8.4.1 Combinations of `for` and `while` loops

You can arbitrarily combine these two types of loops in both BASIC and C. The following program shows how we might do this in BASIC:

```
10 WHILE A%<20
20 A%=A%+1
30 PRINT "PASS NUMBER";A%
40 '
50 FOR B%=1 TO 15
60 PRINT B%;
70 NEXT B%
80 WEND
```

And here is the corresponding C version:

```c
main()
{
    int a = 0;
    int b;
    while (a < 20)
    {
        ++a;
        for(b = 1; b <= 15; ++b);
            printf("%d\n", b);
    }
    gemdos(0x1);
}
```

Both of the programs fill twenty screen lines with the numbers from one to fifteen.

This example shows you how simply the two types of loop can be combined in whatever ways you like.

8.4.2 Nested `while` loops

`while` loops can be nested as easily as `for` loops. We have here a program to demonstrate this.

First the BASIC version:

```
10 WHILE A%<8
20 WHILE B%<2
30 B%=B%+1
40 PRINT A%, B%
50 WEND
55 '
60 B%=0
70 A%=A%+2
80 PRINT "OUTER LOOP"
90 WEND
```

Now the C version:

```
main()
{
    int a, b;
    a = b = 0;
    while(a < 8)
    {
        while(b < 2)
        {
            ++b;
            printf("%d %d\n", a, b);
        }
        b = 0;
        a = a + 2;
        printf("Outer loop\n");
    }
    gemdos(0x1);
}
```

8.4.3 The `do-while` loop

The `do-while` loop is a special form of the normal `while` loop. With this construction, the condition of the loop is checked at the end of the loop instead of the beginning.

A BASIC program would simulate this as follows:

```
10 FOR A=1 TO 2 STEP 0
20 B=B+1
30 PRINT B
40 IF B=100 THEN END
50 NEXT A
```

BASIC does not have the option of a `do-while` loop. It was therefore simulated in this program using an infinite loop. In this loop, the variable a "counts" from 1 to infinity.

The end of the loop is tested in the simulated `do-while` loop with the `IF` line. This statement ends the program when the value of the variable B reaches 100.

Now we come to the C version of the `do-while` loop. The above BASIC program can be written quite simply as follows:

```
main()
{
    int a = 0;
    do
    {
        ++a;
        printf("%d\n", a);
    } while (a <= 100);
    gemdos(0x1);
}
```

Here the `while` condition is found at the end of the statement block which was introduced with `do`. The do statements are repeated as long as the `while` condition is true. When the `while` condition becomes false, the compiler leaves the loop and continues with the program.

It is important to note that the commands within the loop are always executed at least once even if the `while` condition is false to begin with.

Our BASIC version works only in the case where the program and the loop are to be ended at the same time. If additional commands followed our C loop, they would be executed, but because of the END statement, this is not true in the BASIC loop.

This leads directly to our next C control structure, the `break` statement.

8.5 `break` for leaving loops

Let's say we have written the following short C program:

```
main()
{
    int b;
    for(b = 1 ;;)
    {
        ++b;
        printf("%d\n", b);
    }
    gemdos(0x1);
}
```

As we already know from the section on `for` loops, this program contains an infinite loop. It counts from one on up using the variable b.

How do you get out of loops like this? If you have looked at the title of this section, you might guess that the `break` statement will be of some help. `break` is very easy to implement in our example.

Now let's look at the modified program:

```c
main()
{
    int b;
    for(b = 1 ;;)
    {
        ++b;
        printf("%d\n", b);
        if(b == 100)
            break;
    }
    printf("Loop broken\n");
    gemdos(0x1);
}
```

This program, expanded with `if` and `break` statements, counts to 100. When this value is reached the `break` statement interrupts the loop and the compiler leaves it and executes the statements which follow.

In our example, the command:

```c
printf("Loop broken\n");
```

is executed.

The `break` statement does not, therefore, correspond to an END command in BASIC, but instead it allows you to leave `for`, `while`, and `do-while` loops at any point in the loop.

In BASIC, we could simulate the C program as follows:

```
10 FOR A=1 TO 2 STEP 0
20      B=B+1
30      PRINT B
40      IF B=100 THEN GOTO 60
50 NEXT A
55 '
60 PRINT "LOOP BROKEN"
```

Here we see that the `break` statement is simulated by a GOTO jump in line 40 which does not end the program, as did the END command in the earlier program. The endless loop is simply exited and the program continues in line 60. This is very poor programming practice in BASIC, however.

8.6 The `continue` statement

The `continue` statement is the opposite of the `break` statement. It causes the next repetition of the current `for`, `while` or `do-while` loop to begin immediately.

This means that if the compiler encounters the `continue` statement inside a loop, the statements following it in the loop are not executed, but instead the loop is started again from the beginning.

Let's take a look at a C program:

```c
main()
{
    int a[5];
    int i;
    a[0] = 15;
    a[1] = -2;
    a[2] = 0;
    a[3] = 12;
    a[4] = -14;
    for(i = 0; i <= 4; ++i)
    {
        if(a[i] <= 0)
        {
            printf("Value is negative!\n");
            continue;
        }

        printf("Value is positive!\n");
    }
    gemdos(0x1);
}
```

First an array of five elements is defined and each element is assigned a positive or negative integer value. In the `for` loop which follows, each element is evaluated and identified as positive or negative.

If an array element is negative, we don't have to check to see if it is positive after the execution of the line

```
printf("Value is negative.\n");
```

we can go right on to check the next element of the array.

The statement

```
continue;
```

causes execution to start back at the top of the `for` loop.

The statement following the `continue`, or

```
printf("Value is positive.\n");
```

in our example, is then executed. It's not a good idea, after all, to first call a number negative and then turn around right away and call it positive!

In BASIC the direct NEXT instruction corresponds roughly to the C `continue` statement.

Compare the C program with the following BASIC version:

```
10 DIM A(5)
20 '
30 FOR I=1 TO 5 STEP 1
40    IF A(I)<= 0 THEN PRINT "VALUE IS
         NEGATIVE!":
       NEXT A:    REM "CONTINUE"
50    PRINT "VALUE IS POSITIVE!"
60 NEXT A
```

8.7 The `goto` jump

Even C offers a `goto` statement, and it is even more flexible than its BASIC counterpart. In BASIC, a large part of the control structure is built around GOTO commands. Frequent use of these statements can lead to unreadable "spaghetti" code, however, in which it is virtually impossible for someone reading the program to tell what is going on.

To prevent this from the start, we have not used any such `goto` statements in our C programs. You will very seldom find a `goto` statement in a C program, and even then only in isolated cases.

Dennis Ritchie, the developer of the C programming language, strongly recommends that the "`goto`" statement not be used at all, or at least as sparingly as possible. You should therefore discipline yourself not to carry all of your GOTO commands over from BASIC to C.

For situations where the circumstances demand the use of `goto` statements in C, the following pages contain a complete description of this control structure.

The ST's Alcyon C development system does not have this statement yet, but the finished commercial version probably will.

8.7.1 The `goto` syntax

As usual, we will start with a BASIC example:

```
10 A%=10
20 PRINT A%
30 A%=A%-1
40 IF A%>0 THEN GOTO 20
```

Translation to C produces the following program:

```
main()
{
    int a = 10;
    20:
    printf("%d\n", a);
    --a;
    if(a > 0)
        goto 20;
    gemdos(0x1);
}
```

Both programs are constructed the same way and both count down from ten to one. As you can see, the `goto` statement in this example works just like the BASIC `GOTO` statement. The command

```
goto 20;
```

causes a direct jump to line 20, which is wherever the label

```
20:
```

is located in our program.

In C, the `goto` labels are seen as names and not as BASIC-like line numbers. You could, in fact, replace the label 20 with a name if you like.

In the following program, the name `IBegin`, short for "If Begin" has replaced 20 as the beginning label of the loop. The program then looks like this:

```
main()
{
    int a = 10;
    IBegin:
        printf("%d\n", a);
        --a;
        if(a > 0)
            goto IBegin;
        gemdos(0x1);
}
```

8.7.2 Avoiding `gotos`

This example also shows why `goto` jumps are extremely rare in C. Our program can be written more effectively and compactly using a `while` loop.

```
main()
{
    int a = 10;
    while(a > 0)
    {
        printf("%d\n", a);
        --a;
    }
    gemdos(0x1);
}
```

Here it is clear that `goto` jumps can almost always be replaced by another loop construction or by functions. Essentially, any program can be written without `goto` statements.

But where can a `goto` actually be useful?

8.7.3 Applications for `goto`

In practice, it has been shown that the most common use of `goto` is to exit several loops in one move. If, for example, you need to escape from a deeply-nested loop structure, then `goto` is very helpful indeed.

You could use `break`, of course, but remember that `break` leaves only the current loop. To escape a deep structure of nested loops, it is more effective to use the `goto` jump than a long, complex series of interconnected `break` statements.

In using `goto`, it is important to note that the jump can take place only within a function. This means that you cannot use `goto` to jump out of a function or from one function to another.

8.8 Conditional execution with `switch`

The `switch` statement checks an expression to see if it matches one of several constants. It therefore allows the computer to select one of a number of alteratives based on the value of an expression.

This control structure corresponds roughly to the ON-GOTO or ON-GOSUB structures in BASIC. Both branching structures are much less flexible than C's `switch` construction. Let's look at this in more detail with an example.

8.8.1 Example

First the BASIC program, then the C version, which uses `switch`:

```
10 INPUT A
20 ON A GOTO 40, 50
30 PRINT "DEFAULT, VALUE IS NOT 1 OR 2": END
40 PRINT "A IS 1": END
50 PRINT "A IS 2": END
```

```c
main()
{
    int a;
    scanf("%d", &a);
    switch(a)
    {
        case 1:
            printf("Value is 1\n");
            break;
        case 2:
            printf("Value is 2\n");
            break;
        default:
            printf("Default, value is not 1 or 2\n");
    }
    gemdos(0x1);
}
```

Both of these programs read in a number from the keyboard and then determine if this number is 1, 2, or neither of these two.

In C, the `switch` statement takes the following form:

```
switch(x)      (initialization)
case y;        (case test)
default        (default case)
```

8.8.2 The `switch` syntax

The `switch` control structure is introduced with the command:

```
switch(a);
```

This determines the expression to be evaluated. Note that the variable or expression inside the parentheses must represent an integer value.

The conditional statements which follow are then assembled into a statement block inside curly braces.

The individual cases are assigned using a format like:

```
case 1:
    printf("Value is 1\n");
```

If the value of the switch expression is 1 then the statements after `case 1:` are executed. Groups of statements following a single `case` statement need not be assembled into statements blocks with curly braces; the statements themselves serve as separators.

If none of the `case` constants match the variable, then the statements after:

```
default:
```

are executed. `default` is optional. If there is no `default` statement and no matching `case` constant in the `switch` structure, then no action at all is taken.

`case` conditions, by the way, do not have to follow in numeric order (1, 2, ..., default) as they do in BASIC. The following unordered sequence of 2, 3, 1, and `default` is also possible:

```
main()
{
    int a;
    scanf("%d", &a);
    switch(a)
    {
        case 2:
            printf("Value is 2\n");
            break;
        case 3:
            printf("Value is 3\n");
            break;
        case 1:
            printf("Value is 1\n");
            break;
        default:
            printf("Value is not 2, 3, or 1\n");
    }
    gemdos(0x1);
}
```

The `switch` command is not limited to numbers, as in the examples so far, but can work with any integer type, like character values.

This is demonstrated in the following program:

```
main()
{
    char c;
    c = 'h';
    switch(c)
    {
        case 'y':
            printf("Character y\n");
            break;
        case 'a':
            printf("Character a\n");
            break;
        case 'h':
            printf("Character h\n");
            break;
    }
    gemdos(0x1);
}
```

The only real difference between this `switch` structure and the previous ones is that the form of the `case` statements is

```
case 'character':
```

rather than

```
case numerical_value:
```

One additional function of `switch` which cannot be accomplished with BASIC's `ON-GOTO` is the possibility of multiple assignments. The following program uses the `case` tests to determine whether or not a character is a digit.

This can be done more efficiently using the ASCII values of the input (see the chapter on screen input/output operations), but the program below serves as a demonstration of this use of the `switch` structure.

```c
main()
{
    char a;
    a = 6;
    switch (a)
    {
        case '0':
        case '1':
        case '2':
        case '3':
        case '4':
        case '5':
        case '6':
        case '7':
        case '8':
        case '9':
            printf("Character is a digit!\n");
            break;
        default:
            printf("Character is a not a digit!\n");
    }
    gemdos(0x1);
}
```

In this program, there is no `break` between the alternatives so the program passes immediately from one to the other.

In general, this can be sketched as follows:

```c
switch (x)
{
    case a:
    case b:
    case c:
        Execute commands when x matches a, b, or c
}
```

Take careful note of the use of `break` statement. Its role in the `switch` structure is very important. If one case is found to be true, it doesn't usually make sense to examine the rest of the cases. The `break` statement is used here in order to avoid this wasteful procedure. Our previous examples are all optimized using `break`.

Chapter 9

Common Mistakes of BASIC Programmers

Common Mistakes of BASIC Programmers

You have now reached a point where you should have a large part of C mastered. Most of all, the relationships between BASIC and C should be clear to you. What we have covered so far is a complete description of the elementary elements of the C programming language.

Before we cover the material in the following chapters in any detail, we should look at some of the most common mistakes which BASIC programmers make. Seeing these typical mistakes now will help you to avoid making them later.

Consider this chapter a quiz. First you will see a program containing one mistake. Following it will be a complete explanation of this error.

Don't read the explanation right away if the answer does not come to you immediately. Look carefully; many mistakes will not be apparent at first.

9.1 Error # 1

```
main()
{
    int x;
    x = 15;
    print("%d",x);
    gemdos(0x1);
}
```

Have you found the error yet? No? At first sight this program seems to be completely in order. This is a typical mistake which can really be made only by someone who has programmed in BASIC. Nobody learning C as his first programming language would make this error (except as a typo).

In case you still haven't noticed, the `print()` function is certainly familiar from BASIC as the `PRINT` statement, but the actual name of the C function is `printf()` and not `print()`. This type of mistake is especially frustrating because it is so difficult to find.

9.2 Error # 2

```
main()
{
    int integer;
    while(integer < 10)
    {
        printf("Value     x^2 value\n");
        printf("%d %d\n", integer, integer * integer);
        ++integer;
    }
    gemdos(0x1);
}
```

This program uses a `while` loop to create a table of the squares of the integers from one to ten. The mistake is again one typical of BASIC programmers.

Look again at the initialization of the variable. After the declaration:

```
int integer;
```

there must be a value assignment before the start of the `while` loop:

```
integer = 0;
```

In BASIC, this is not necessary because the values of all variables are automatically set to zero by the RUN command. In C, however, you must never forget to set the initial value of every variable before it is used.

This can be done with the combined declaration/assignment statement, as you know:

```
int integer = 0;
```

9.3 Error # 3

```
main()
{
    int integer;
    for(integer = 0; integer <= 10; ++integer);
    {
        printf("Value   x^2 value\n");
        printf("%d %d\n", integer, integer * integer);
    }
    gemdos(0x1);
}
```

This program corresponds exactly to the previous one, except that the loop is created using `for` instead of `while`.

Have you found the mistake yet? You might guess that there would be a problem because the variable `integer` is not initialized before the loop. It is initialized *inside* the loop, however, so this is not necessary.

Again, the error is rather subtle. Remember that a semicolon in C separates statements, so that when the compiler sees a semicolon it thinks that the statement is over and goes on to the next one. The `for` statement in C is viewed by the compiler as exactly one statement even though the `for` loop may contain hundreds of other statements. The curly braces make the compiler treat the whole loop as one statement. So the problem here is that the `for` loop is really over before we get to the statements that it is supposed to repeat. The instructions between the braces after the `for` statement are not repeated but are executed only once. To fix this, remove the semicolon after the `for` loop declaration.

9.4 Error #4

```
main()
{
    int value;
    scanf("%d", &value);
    if(value = 15)
        printf("15 is the answer!\n");
    else
        printf("That's not it!\n");
    gemdos(0x1);
}
```

This one may also have been difficult for you. It really looks completely normal to a BASIC programmer.

Look more carefully at the `if` statement. In the previous chapters we said that the assignment operator = must not be confused with the equality comparison operator ==. The correct `if` statement would then read `if(value == 15)` rather than `if(value = 15)`.

9.5 Error #5

```
main()
{
    int value_1, value_2;
    value_1 = 15;
    value_2 = 3.5;
    printf("%d\n", value_1 * value_2);
    gemdos(0x1);
}
```

Here the variables `value_1` and `value_2` are declared, assigned values, and multiplied together. Their product is then printed on the screen.

Have you noticed where the mistake is?

The error lies in the value assignments. Because `value_2` was declared as an integer, just like `value_1`, it cannot be assigned the floating-point value 3.5.

This program would run on most compilers, but with the unwanted side effect that `value_2` would be assigned the integer value of 3.5, which is 3.

If, however, you want the value 3.5 to be used, you must first declare `value_2` as a `float` variable. Next, the `printf` call must be changed. Instead of `%d`, you must write `%f` for the number to be printed as floating-point.

9.6 Error #6

```
main()
{
    a = 15;
    printf("%d\n", a);
    gemdos(0x1);
}
```

Here we see another typical BASIC error. At first glance, the program looks correct. There are no errors in the `printf` call and the braces around the function `main()` are placed correctly. The value assignment of the variable `a` is also in order.

There is, however, a mistake here. In BASIC, it is not necessary to declare a variable, but it must never be forgotten in C. Insert the line

```
int a;
```

or

```
float a;
```

depending on whether the variable a should be treated as an integer or a floating-point number, and the program is complete.

9.7 Error #7

```
main()
{
    printf("%f\n", 1 / 3);
    gemdos(0x1);
}
```

What? This program is wrong? Are you trying to trick me?

If you don't believe that the above program contains an error, just run it through your C compiler and you will receive the (incorrect!) output

```
0.000000
```

or maybe even an error.

The error can only lie in the `printf` call. This should print out the fraction 1/3. The output format is also correctly set at `%f`.

As we have already stressed in the chapter on screen input and output, however, the numbers 1 and 3 must be written specifically as floating-point values rather than as integers.

The correct program looks like this:

```
main()
{
    printf("%f\n", 1.0 / 3.0);
    gemdos(0x1);
}
```

9.8 Error #8

```
main()
    int a, b, c, d;
    scanf("%d", &a);
    b = a + 6;
    c = b * 4;
    d = b - c;
    printf("%d %d %d %d\n", a, b, c, d);
    gemdos(0x1);
}
```

Many of you probably noticed this error right away. The problem with this error is that the compiler will generate several different error messages, none of which give the specific reason for the error.

In this example, the first curly brace after the `main()` function declaration is missing. In this short program, the mistake was easy to find. In larger programs, however, it may be exceptionally difficult to find these errors due to the misleading error messages.

When you think about it, a large program would not consist of a single block of commands, but would instead have a complex series of them, intermixed and nested within one another to the point where it would be very easy to leave a brace out.

When you suspect that you have left a brace off a block somewhere deep in a confusing series of nested loops you'll have to decide yourself where you should look, because the compiler is not going to give you very helpful error messages.

9.9 Error #9

```
main()
{
    int loop;
    for(loop = 1; loop =< 10; ++loop)
    {
        printf("%d %d\n", loop, loop * 2);
    }
    gemdos(0x1);
}
```

Granted, the error is hard to find.

Look more carefully at the `for` loop definition. The error is found in the condition `loop  =<  10;`. In a few BASIC versions, the comparison operator =< is permissible, but not in C.

The correct version must read `loop <= 10;`.

Just remember that the equals sign always comes last in the "less than or equal to" and "greater than or equal to" operators, resulting in <= and >=.

9.10 Error #10

```
main()
{
    int x;
    scanf("%d", x);
    printf("%d %d\n", x, x * x);
    gemdos(0x1);
}
```

Again, at first glance there seems to be no mistake hidden in this program... or is there? How did that go with the `scanf` function again?

If you didn't notice the error immediately, do you remember now? `scanf` always needs a pointer to tell the computer where in memory it should place the value it reads in.

The correct `scanf` call changes the integer variable to a pointer variable with the address operator & and looks like this:

```
scanf("%d", &x);
```

9.11 Error #11

```
main()
{
    int a, b, c, d;
    a = b = 15;
    for(c = a, d = c * 2; a < 5; a++, d++)
    {
        printf("%d\n", a);
        c = a * 12;
        b = c - a;
        printf("%d %d\n", c, b);

    gemdos(0x1);

}
```

Don't let this program confuse you. The nature of this error is very simple. It does not lie in the `for` statement, although this is extended with the comma operator.

You will find the error immediately if you again look at the information given on the brace structure in error number 8. To be precise, the bracket at the end of the `for` loop has been left out. This must be inserted after the last `printf` statement.

9.12 Error #12

```
main()
{
    int a, d;
    float b;
    char *c;
    scanf("%d %f %s", &a, &b, &c);
    for(d = 1; d < a; ++d)
        printf("%s\n", c);
    gemdos(0x1);
}
```

This program reads in a string, an integer, and a floating-point number, and uses a `for` loop to print out the string a times on the screen.

This time the `scanf` call contains the error. If you have not yet found the error, look more carefully at this statement. The string variable `c` has already been declared as a pointer and therefore does not need the address operator to make it one. The correct call is as follows:

```
scanf("%d %f %s", &a, &b, c);
```

9.13 Error #13

```
main()
{
    char *string;
    string = "||";
    printf(%s "Error", string);
    gemdos(0x1);
}
```

This program should print the message

    ||Error

on the screen.

In its present form, however, the program will not do it. This is because the `%s` expression is inside the `printf` call. This and all other data type assignments for printing must always be inside the quotation marks.

The corrected line reads:

    printf("%s Error", string);

9.14 Error #14

```
main()
{
    printf("There is a future\n in programming\n
            in C!\n");
    gemdos(0x1);
}
```

Does this program have an error or not? Try it out!

Although this looks strange, it runs without a problem. It prints three lines:

    There is a future
    in programming
    in C!

one after the other on the screen.

The new line marker \n, which represents the end of a line, can be put anywhere in a string, not just at the end of a line.

9.15 Error #15

```
main()
{
    int x;
    for(x = 10; x > 0; --x)
        printf("%d\n", x)
    gemdos(0x1);
}
```

Have you found the error yet? If not, you will probably kick yourself when you finally discover it.

This is an error most often caused by haste, and every C programmer makes it at some point, but BASIC programmers are especially prone to it.

For the solution, look more carefully at the `printf` call in the `for` loop. This line is simply missing its semicolon.

In BASIC, we would not have to use a statement separator here. You must always remember that the semicolon must be used to separate individual statements from one another. In that respect, it corresponds to the colon in BASIC, but the semicolon must follow every statement in C (remember that the `printf` call is really part of the `for` statement).

9.16 Error #16

```
main()
{
    int x = 10;
    while(x > 0)
    {
        printf("The number is %d"\n,x);
        --x;
    }
    gemdos(0x1);
}
```

This program counts down from ten to one.

The error is in the `printf` call. The new-line control character "\n", like all other control characters, must be inside the quotation marks.

The correct call reads as follows:

```
printf("The number is %d\n",x);
```

This example also shows how to print out strings and numeric variables together, using one call. This is more efficient than two separate `printf` calls. Remember this structure because you will certainly use it often in your programs.

9.17 Error #17

```
main()
{
    int x;
    scanf("%d\n", &x);
    printf("%d %d\n", x, x*x*x);
    gemdos(0x1);
}
```

Here we have a logical error in the `scanf` input call. Take another look at this statement.

Do you notice anything unusual? The control character \n is completely out of place in this statement.

This error can occur because `scanf` and `printf` are almost identical in their syntax, and `printf` very often uses the new-line character \n. The `scanf` function, however, has no reason to look for this character because the new-line after the input is automatic.

The correct line must read:

```
scanf("%d", &x);
```

Some compilers, like Alcyon C, ignore the misplaced new-line character and therefore produce no error.

9.18 Error #18

```
main()
{
    int a, b;
    char *c;
        a = b = 15;
        c = "DIGITAL GEM";
    printf("%d %s %d\n", a, b, c);
    gemdos(0x1);
}
```

The error in this program is a difficult one to find. Again, it is in the `printf` call. If you compare the data type control characters with the corresponding variables, you will quickly see that the variable b is of type integer, but that it will be printed out as a string. Likewise, the `printf` function tries to print the string variable c as %d, an integer.

It is important to avoid these mistakes because they don't usually generate error messages, just incorrect output. Always be careful to use the correct data-type control characters.

The correct `printf` call must read:

```
printf("%d %d %s\n", a, b, c);
```

9.19 Error #19

```
main()
{
    int x, y;
    scanf("%d", &x);
    y = 14;
    if (x <> y)
        printf("The x-value is not equal to the
                y-value!\n");
        else
        printf("The x-value is equal to the
                y-value\n");
    gemdos(0x1);
}
```

The error here is very typical of BASIC programmers, but you have enough C experience that you should find it right away.

The mistake is in the if statement if(x <> y). The BASIC inequality symbol is indeed <>, but in C it is !=.

The if statement is written correctly as

```
if(x != y)
```

Chapter 10

C Functions

C Functions

As we said before, most C programs consist of a set of individual functions. A function is a subprogram, comparable to subroutines in BASIC which are called with GOSUB and ended with RETURN.

Even though C does not require you to use functions, it is not good programming style to put all of your commands in one procedure (that is, in the main() function) as is often the case in BASIC. Instead, you should divide your program into separate functions which are called from main().

You will soon get used to this new programming style. Forget your BASIC programming structure. Your C programs will be much easier to read and understand if you build them up out of individual functions. Also, it is much less complicated to change a program that is divided into functions than one which is just a mass of statements.

One of the primary advantages of functions is that you can use what are called "standard functions." Once created, these functions can be used in any program.

This is the main reason that functions play such an important role in C. Functions allow you to virtually write your own programming language. The C language itself is really quite compact and has relatively few commands. Functions, however, extend the language greatly and handle all of the machine-dependent tasks such as input/output.

The C compiler libraries on the Atari ST are really nothing more than functions which you can access. To use GEM in your C programs, for example, all you have to do is link the corresponding libraries to your program. The libraries then provide a large supply of useful functions for you to use in your programs.

Naturally this raises some questions: How are these functions constructed? How are they included in programs? How are they called from the programs?

We will answer these and other questions in the following pages, using many BASIC and C examples.

10.1 Fundamentals of functions

Any C program can contain an arbitrary number of functions. At least one function is required in every program. This is the function

```
main()
```

This function represents the program head; and it is always the first function called when the program is executed. The general procedure is then to call all of the other functions from `main()` so that the program is not actually located in this main function, but the operations take place in the individual subroutines. The function `main()` is therefore used primarily to manage and call the other functions.

10.1.1 Calling functions

Take a look at the following example. In this example, the function `main()` calls itself again.

```
main()
{
    printf("Hello, how are you?\n");
    main();
}
```

This program prints the following output:

```
Hello, how are you?
Hello, how are you?
Hello, how are you?
Hello, how are you?
Hello, how are you?
Hello, how are you?
Hello, how are you?
...
```

The text is printed on the screen over and over again.

Press <CTRL> C to end the program and return to C again.

In this example, the function `main()` calls itself with:

    main();

A function is generally called by placing its name in the program. Parameters can be passed to the function by enclosing them in parentheses after the function name. Since `main` doesn't take any parameters here, there is nothing between them. The parentheses themselves must be included, however.

10.1.2 Functions without parameters

Now let's use the facts we have mentioned in a demonstration program. Here is a BASIC example:

```
10 PRINT "BASIC"
20 GOSUB 1000
30 '
40 PRINT "FORTH"
50 GOSUB 1000
60 '
70 PRINT "LISP"
80 GOSUB 1000
90 '
100 PRINT "PROLOG"
110 GOSUB 1000
120 '
130 PRINT "C"
140 GOSUB 1000
150 END
160 '
1000 REM SUBROUTINE "KEYSTOP"
1005 '
1010 PRINT "PRESS A KEY..."
1020 GET A$
1030 IF A$="" THEN 1020
1035 '
1040 RETURN
```

This program prints the names of several programming languages, one after the other. After each language, the program uses GOSUB to jump to the subroutine KEYSTOP, in which the message:

    PRESS A KEY...

appears on the screen and the computer waits for a keystroke. When a key is pressed, the RETURN command restores control to the main program.

Now compare the BASIC program with the following C version:

```
#include "stdio.h"
#define getchar() getc(stdin)
main()
{
    printf("BASIC\n");
    keystop();
    printf("FORTH\n");
    keystop();
    printf("LISP\n");
    keystop();
    printf("PROLOG\n");
    keystop();
    printf("C\n");
    keystop();
    gemdos(0x1);
}
keystop()
{
    int a;
    printf("Press a key...\n");
    getch(a);
}
char bf[100];
int b = 0;
getch()
{
    return((b > 0) ? bf[--b] : getchar());
}
```

In this program, you see the function `keystop` called from the main program `main()` with the statement:

```
keystop();
```

The first thing this function does is to define a local variable of type integer. Next, the message:

```
Press a key...
```

is printed out and the program then uses the call `getch(a)` to wait for a key to be pressed on the keyboard. The return of control to the calling program is then automatic. In Digital C, however, `return` must be specified explicitly.

As you can see, there aren't too many differences between BASIC and C routines. In C, a function is called simply using the function name, whereas in BASIC, the line number of the first command of the subroutine is used.

It is not necessary to use `return` to end a function in C. The return to the calling function is performed automatically after the last statement in the function has been executed. In our case, control was returned to the function `main()` after the statement `getch(a);`.

We could have formulated the function `keystop` in a number of different ways. We could have written a PAUSE function, or a WAIT instruction as it is implemented in some versions of BASIC.

The BASIC example would then read:

```
1000 REM PAUSE SUBROUTINE "KEYSTOP"
1005 :
1010 PAUSE 1000
1020 RETURN
```

or, if your BASIC does not include the PAUSE n command, as follows:

```
1000 REM PAUSE SUBROUTINE "KEYSTOP"
1005 :
1010 FOR A=1 TO 10000: NEXT A
1020 RETURN
```

Both subprograms produce a certain time delay before the next programming language is printed out.

In C, the corresponding function would look like this:

```
keystop()
{
    int x;
    for(x = 1; x < 30000; ++x)
        ;
}
```

This pause routine, as well as the previous keystroke function, can be put to use in your own programs.

10.1.3 Functions calling each other

Look at the following C program:

```
main()
{
    M();
    gemdos(0x1);
}
e()
{
    putchar('e');
    s();
    putchar('!');
}

M()
{
    putchar('M');
    e();
}
s()
{
    printf("ss");
}
```

In this example, it becomes clear how functions in C can call each other.

This can also be done in BASIC. The above C program looks something like this in BASIC:

```
10 GOSUB 100
20 END
30 '
100 PRINT "M";
110 GOSUB 200
120 RETURN
130 '
200 PRINT "E";
210 GOSUB 300
220 PRINT "!";
230 RETURN
240 '
300 PRINT "SS";
310 RETURN
```

Have you figured out what these programs do? Consistent with the nature of the programs and their function calls, the outputs of the C and BASIC programs are:

    Mess!

and

    MESS!

respectively. In this example you can see how C functions can be called by and nested within each another.

10.2 Passing parameters to functions

Up to now, C functions have not seemed much different from subroutines in BASIC. This is only because we have not started passing parameters yet.

This case was shown in the examples on the previous pages. The function `keystop()`, called from `main()`, generates only a fixed time delay.

Assume, for example, that you want to simulate a

```
PAUSE n
```

command like the one already found in BASIC.

To accomplish this in C, the parameter n must be passed to the function.

The function then looks like this:

```
pause(n);
int n;
{
    int a;
    for(a = 1; a < n; ++a)
        ;
}
```

The n in the parentheses after `pause` tells it that it should accept a parameter passed to it and call it n.

The function is called with a statement like

```
pause(10000);
```

or

```
pause(40000);
```

or `pause(n)` with any other number. This makes the `for` loop longer or shorter, corresponding exactly to the BASIC command.

Let's look at our new `pause(n)` function more closely in an example program:

```
main()
{
    printf("Hello, ");
    pause(30000);
    printf("how");
    pause(20000);
    printf(" are you?\n");
    gemdos(0x1);
}
pause(n);
int n;
{
    int a;
    for (a = 1; a < n; ++a)
    ;
}
```

As another opportunity for comparison, here is the corresponding program in BASIC.

We will assume here that the version of BASIC we are using does not include the PAUSE n command and must therefore be written as follows:

```
10 PRINT "HELLO, ";
20 N=3000: GOSUB 1000
25 '
30 PRINT "HOW";
40 N=2000: GOSUB 1000
45 '
50 PRINT " ARE YOU?"
60 END
65 '
1000 REM PAUSE N
1010 FOR A=1 TO N: NEXT A
1020 RETURN
```

In BASIC it is not possible to pass parameters directly. As in this example, they must be passed indirectly using global variables.

In this case, the variable N represents the length of the pause, which controls the FOR-NEXT loop in the subroutine starting at line 1000.

10.2.1 Returning integer data

So far we have covered the format of functions, how they call each other, and how parameters are passed.

If, however, you want the function to return a value to the calling function, you must follow a procedure which is somewhat unusual compared to BASIC.

Let's take the following program, which computes the cube of a number, as an example:

```
10 INPUT X%
20 GOSUB 100
30 PRINT Y%
40 END
50 '
100 Y% = X% * X% * X%
110 RETURN
```

We write a corresponding C program using two functions:

```
main()
{
    int x, y;
    scanf("%d", &x);
    y = cube(x);
    printf("The cube of X is %d\n", y);
    gemdos(0x1);
}
cube(z)
int z;
{
    return(z * z * z);
}
```

In C, the value of x^3 must be returned to `main()` using the `return` statement.

The statement

```
y = cube(x);
```

assigns to `y` the exact value which appears between the parentheses in the `return` statement in `cube`. This is hard to get used to, especially for BASIC programmers, but it offers advantages which will become obvious by the end of the chapter.

For comparison, let me show you an example of how functions may *not* be used:

```
main()
{
    int x, y;
    scanf("%d", &x);
    y = square(x);

    printf("%d\n", y);
    gemdos(0x1);
}

square(q)
int q;
{
    q = q * q;
}
```

This program illustrates an error very typical of BASIC programmers. In BASIC, a subroutine structured like this would run without a problem, but not in C. Why?

The procedure changes only the value of a variable, but does not permanently assign the new value to a memory address. To accomplish this, you use the `return` statement as before.

In this book we have learned another way to assign variable values to specific memory addresses. This is done with pointer variables. In a few pages we will explain how you can use pointers to arbitrarily exchange values between functions without using the `return` statement.

10.2.2 Returning other numerical data types

When we want a function to return a variable type other than integer, we have to make a change. To explain this, let's change our previous BASIC program so that the number to be cubed doesn't have to be an integer, but can also be a floating-point variable.

```
10 INPUT X
20 GOSUB 100
30 PRINT Y
40 END
50 '
100 Y = X * X * X
110 RETURN
```

The C version would then read:

```
main()
{
    float x, y, cube();
    scanf("%d", &x);
    y = cube(x);
    printf("The cube of X is %d\n", y);
    gemdos(0x1);
}
float cube(z)
float z;
{
    return(z * z * z);
}
```

As you can see, the function name must be declared as `float` at the beginning of the function `main()` if it is to return a floating-point number.

This is done with the declaration statement

```
float cube();
```

This variable type must then be declared in the function `cube()`. Again, this is not necessary for integer values.

Notice that the function was no longer introduced with just the simple function name

```
cube(z)
```

but with the function header

```
float cube(z)
```

You must therefore declare the variable type again before the function name. In practice, however, you will find or actually use very few `float` functions in C programs. Instead, most functions which do not return integer values will be declared as "`double`" functions in order to take advantage of the increased accuracy of this variable type.

10.2.3 Pointers, functions, and simultaneous parameter passing

Pointers play a very important role in transferring data between functions. Let's look at how pointers are used, starting with a BASIC program.

```
10   INPUT A
20   INPUT B
30   GOSUB 1000
40   PRINT A;B
50   END
100  '
1000 REM SWAP
1010 HI=A
1020 A=B
1030 B=HI
1040 RETURN
```

Here, the subroutine `SWAP` exchanges the values of the variables `A` and `B`. Some versions of BASIC include a special `SWAP` command for this purpose. This, if it is offered, corresponds exactly to the subroutine above. A command like this is very useful, and is used in sorting routines, among others.

Now we come to the C version, which uses pointers:

```
main()
{
    int a, b;
    scanf("%d %d", &a, &b);
    swap(&a, &b);
    printf("%d %d\n", a, b);
    gemdos(0x1);
}
swap(c, d)
int *c, *d;
{
    int temp;
    temp = *c;
    *c = *d;
    *d = temp;
}
```

A comparison between the C and BASIC subroutines quickly reveals how much alike they are. Using pointers, you can write subroutines in C in almost the same way you would in BASIC.

The only real difference is the declaration of pointers. You must, of course, declare all local variables within a function as usual.

Pointers have already been thoroughly explained in this book. To avoid repeating this material, we will restrict ourselves to a brief explanation of the specific uses of pointers in transferring values between functions, using this program as an example.

First, let's look at the call to the `swap` function in the line

```
swap(&a, &b);
```

The variables a and b must always be preceded by the address operator & because the values in the function `swap()` are to be changed using memory addresses. The memory addresses of the variables are passed to `swap` via &a and &b.

Inside the called function, the variables c and d must be declared as integer pointers so that they can receive the contents of the pointers &a and &b from main(). The values in the two pointer addresses are then exchanged. The variable temp which is used for this purpose need not be a pointer.

The two altered variables are then returned to the function main() as integer pointers. The contents of the variables a and b are thus swapped.

In this example, we passed two parameters to a function and got two values back as well. return can pass back only one value. Only the use of pointers allows us to return more than one value.

As we have already mentioned, the development version of the Alcyon C on the Atari ST does not perform pointer operations correctly, so this function won't work properly with this compiler.

The non-standard pointer operations are the biggest fault of this compiler, and certainly must be fixed before the commercial version can be considered ready. On all other compilers, the pointer operators function as described above.

10.3 The DEF FN command

In BASIC it is possible to define functions using DEF FN. The following example program defines and performs a cube function.

```
10 DEF FNCUBE(X) = X*X*X
20 '
30 INPUT X:
40 Y=FNCUBE(X): PRINT Y
50 END
```

In C, we can define a function using the `#define` construction, which we have already used to create symbolic constants. Our BASIC program is then changed in C to:

```
#define cube(x) x * x * x
main()
{
    int x, y;
    scanf("%d", &x);
    y = cube(x);
    printf("The cube of X is %d\n", y);
    gemdos(0x1);
}
```

Here the statement:

```
#define cube(x) x * x * x
```

is what is called a *macro*. Macros are quick and easy to write. Their biggest advantages are their flexibility and uncomplicated structure.

Compare the `cube` macro with the corresponding conventional function:

```
cube(z)
int z;
{
    return(z * z * z);
}
```

As you can see, this function is larger and less efficient than the macro. Because of this, macros are found quite often in C programs.

How does a macro work? This method of constructing functions is identical to the symbolic constants described earlier in this book. There, we said that the compiler substitutes the contents of the `#define` expression wherever the corresponding name appears.

This allows us to write anything as a macro, not just functions. This includes statements and function calls, as is shown in the following example:

```
#define printfs(x) printf("%s\n", x);
main()
{
    char *a;
    a = "Input...>";

    printfs(a);
    gemdos(0x1);
}
```

Chapter 11

Structures

Structures

Structures are not available in BASIC, but they are available in many other programming languages. In Pascal, for example, this variable type is called a record.

In the following pages, we will describe everything important for you to know as a BASIC programmer—the syntax of structures and how they are used in programs.

To reassure you, we would like to make something clear from the start. In our opinion, structures are not all that important for BASIC programmers at the beginning. As we have already mentioned, any C program can be written without them, using only the customary variable types.

As your experience and knowledge of C grow, you will find that complicated algorithms can be simplified and made more readable using structures.

11.1 Declaring structures

What are structures? *Structures* allow us to group together several variables of different types so that we can access them under one name. We use arrays to associate items of the same type together and structures allow us to associate items of differing types.

The declaration takes place in its own routine. Take a look at the following example:

```
struct item
{
    int quantity;
    char *description;
    float price;
};
```

The declaration of `item` sets up a structure which might be used in an inventory. The individual elements of the structure are the quantity, description, and price of the item.

The example, when written out, makes it clear why we have referred to structures as a way of associating variables. The structure name `item` applies to all of the names which are defined under it.

This type of structure declaration normally takes place at the beginning of a program, before global or local variables are defined. Note the semicolon which follows the declaration--it must always follow the closing bracket.

11.2 Use of structure variables

Let's stay with our item example. The form of the structure `item` is determined through the above declaration. In other words, we have declared that the first element of the structure represents the `quantity`, the second the `description`, and the third the `price`. In a table, it looks like this:

```
FORM: quantity(int)    description(*char)    price(float)
-----------------------------------------------------------------
item no.1    ...                ...                ...
item no.2    ...                ...                ...
item no.3    ...                ...                ...
   ...
item no.n    ...                ...                ...
```

The first line of the chart represents the form of the structure `item`, which was determined by the previous structure declaration. As is shown in the left column, this form can be used with an arbitrary number of items.

The number of items you want and exactly how they should be addressed as variables, are determined in the structure variable declaration. If, for example, only three items (no_1 through no_3) are to be declared as variables of the structure, then the following notation is necessary.

```
struct item no_1, no_2, no_3;
```

This table shows how the individual variables are addressed later in the program:

```
       number(int)      description(*char)    price(float)
     -----------------------------------------------------------
       no_1.quantity    no_1.description      no_1.price
       no_2.quantity    no_2.description      no_2.price
       no_3.quantity    no_3.description      no_3.price
```

Here you can see how the individual elements of the structure item are accessed. The general form is

```
       structure_variable_name.element_name
```

First you must give the structure variable name, in this case, no_1, no_2, or no_3, followed by a period and the name of the element from the structure declaration must be included. In our example, these elements are quantity, description, and price.

Structure variables formulated in this manner can be used just like normal variables. For example:

```
       no_2.quantity = 125;
```

or

```
       no_1.description = "ATARI 520ST";
```

This short example program demonstrates how structure elements are used in a program:

```
   struct item
   {
       int quantity;
       char *description;
       float price;
   };
   main()
   {
       struct item no_1, no_2, no_3;
       no_1.quantity = 125;
       no_1.description = "ATARI 520ST";
       no_1.price = 699.0;
       no_2.quantity = 15;
```

```
            no_2.description = "Commodore C-128";
            no_2.price = 279.0;

            no_3.quantity = 548;
            no_3.description = "Amiga";
            no_3.price = 1295.0;

            printf("The quantity of the first item is %d\n",no_1.quantity);
            printf("The second item is a %s\n",no_2.description);
            printf("The price of the first item is %f\n",no_1.price);
            gemdos(0x1);
        }
```

Two things are shown in the `main()` function of this program. First, we once again show how structure variable are declared, and second, we show how elements of structures are used in a program.

11.3 Arrays and structures

You can now use structures and structure variables in your programs without problems. In this section, you will learn how to simplify working with structure variables. In the previous example, the structure variable names were labeled `no_1`, `no_2`, and `no_3`.

In practice, things are almost never done this way. The articles can be addressed more efficiently using arrays.

The structure variable declaration in the `main()` function looks like this with an array:

```
        struct item no[3];
```

instead of the original

```
        struct item no_1, no_2, no_3;
```

Arrays make it much easier to access structure variables from a large group of them.

Our table would then be changed to:

```
quantity(int)    description(*char)    price(float)
-----------------------------------------------------
no[1].quantity   no[1].description     no[1].price
no[2].quantity   no[2].description     no[2].price
no[3].quantity   no[3].description     no[3].price
```

Now let's extend our previous program using an array:

```c
struct item
{
    int quantity;
    char *description
    float price;
};
main()
{
    int n;
    struct item no[3];

    no[1].quantity = 125;
    no[1].description = "ATARI 520ST";
    no[1].price = 699.0;

    no[2].quantity = 15;
    no[2].description = "Commodore C-128";
    no[2].price = 279.0;

    no[3].quantity = 548;
    no[3].description = "Amiga";
    no[3].price = 1295.0;

    printf("Quantity Description Price\n");
    for(n=0; n < 3; ++n)
    {
       printf("%d    %s    %f\n", no[n].quantity,
              no[n].description, no[n].price);
    }
    gemdos(0x1);
}
```

In this example it becomes clear why nearly all structures are defined as arrays.

The `for` loop, which prints out all of the elements of a structure, can be used only with the help of arrays. This makes possible the generalized calls:

```
no[n].number

no[n].description
```

and

```
no[n].price
```

Using arrays of structures also makes it easier to change the program later. For example, if you want to change the number of items in our program from 3 to 100, all you have to do is change the number in the declaration.

The declaration:

```
struct item no[3];
```

would then be changed to:

```
struct item no[100];
```

After you have tried out the example programs, experiment with structures in your own programs to reinforce your knowledge.

Chapter 12

An Overview of C

A C overview

12.1 Keywords in C

The following pages contain a brief summary of the most important C language elements.

LOOP INSTRUCTIONS

```
for
do
while
```

DECISION INSTRUCTIONS

```
if
else
switch
case
default
```

JUMP INSTRUCTIONS

```
break
continue
goto
```

STORAGE CLASSES

```
auto
extern
static
```

DATA TYPES

```
int
short
long
unsigned
float
double
char
struct
```

OTHER EXPRESSIONS

```
return
exit
type
define
include
printf
scanf
```

These key words, especially important for those learning C, represent the language's core vocabulary. You can see that this fundamental vocabulary is considerably smaller than that of BASIC.

In the following sections we discuss the core statements of the language.

12.2 C language statements

In this summary you will get one last look at the important language elements and their syntax and how they are implemented in C programs.

12.2.1 The `break` statement

Syntax:

```
break;
```

The `break` statement is used whenever a `do`, `for`, `switch`, or `while` statement should be stopped immediately. After the `break` jump, the program resumes running after the loop or `switch` statement, as the case may be.

12.2.2 The `case` statement

Syntax:

```
case constant:
    statement 1;
    statement 2;
    ...
```

The `case` statement is a component element of the `switch` branching structure. If the constant in the `case` statement matches the `switch` expression, then the statements within the `case` block are executed.

12.2.3 The `continue` statement

Syntax:

```
continue;
```

The `continue` statement is used inside a loop. If this statement is encountered, none of the statements which follow it in the loop are executed. Instead, the next pass through the loop is begun.

12.2.4 The `#define` statement

Syntax 1:

```
#define name replacement_text
```

When this statement is used at the beginning of a C program, `name` will be replaced by the replacement text wherever `name` is encountered after the definition in program.

Syntax 2:

```
#define name(param_1, param_2, ...param_n) text
```

The macro `name` is defined and places the n parameters in the `text` statement, which is substituted for `name` in the program. One example is the macro

```
#define square(x) x * x
```

The macro is called with a statement like

```
x = square(value_1 * 2);
```

which is replaced with

```
x = (value_1 * 2) * (value_1 * 2);
```

12.2.5 The `default` statement

Syntax:

```
default:
    program expression;
```

the `default` statement causes the statements following it to be carried out within a `switch` structure when none of the preceding `case` statements match the `switch` expression.

If a `switch` structure contains no `default` statement and none of the `case` conditions are fulfilled, nothing is executed.

12.2.6 The `do` statement

Syntax:

```
do
{
    statements
}
while (condition)
```

The program statements within the do loop are executed as long as the condition in the `while` statement is true.

It should be noted that statements within the do loop are executed at least once because the `while` condition is not checked until the end of the loop.

12.2.7 The **else** statement

Syntax:

```
else
    statement;
```

The else statement is a component of the if structure. The else statement (which may also be a statement block) is executed when the if condition is false, or logically equal to zero.

12.2.8 The **else if** statement

Syntax:

```
else if(condition)
    statement;
```

The else if statement follows an if statement or another else if. If the else if condition is true, or logically unequal to zero, the statement (block) following it will be executed.

12.2.9 The **for** statement

Syntax:

```
for(first interval bound, second bound, step size)
    statement;
```

The first interval bound initializes a loop variable. This value determines the lower boundary of the loop. The second bound sets the condition for the end of the for loop.

The step size determines the change made in the loop variable each time the loop is executed. The statement is repeated within the loop.

12.2.10 The `goto` statement

Syntax:

```
goto label;
```

The execution of the `goto` statement causes a direct jump to the position within the program which is identified by

```
label: statement
```

12.2.11 The `if` statement

Syntax:

```
if(condition)
    statement;
```

If the condition is true, or logically unequal to zero, the statement will be executed.

12.2.12 The null statement

Syntax:

```
;
```

This expression does absolutely nothing while the program is running. It must often be used, however, to fill in the requirements of the specific syntax of some statements (for example, in `do`, `for`, and `while` loops).

An example of its use is a delay loop like the following:

```
for(a = 1; a < 1000; ++a)
    ;
```

12.2.13 The `return` statement

Syntax 1:

```
return;
```

The `return` statement causes an immediate jump from the function in which it is located back to the calling function. This instruction is not necessary if the function is to end when the last statement is executed.
Syntax 2:

```
return (expression);
```

The value of the expression is returned to the function name.

12.2.14 The `struct` statement

Syntax:

```
struct name
{
    variable declaration 1
    variable declaration 2
    ...
    variable declaration n
};

struct name variable 1, variable 2, ..., variable n;
```

First, the structure variable name is declared with n variables. The variables may be of any type. Before it can be used in a program, variable names must be assigned the structure's form.

Structure elements are accessed in a program as follows:

First the name of the structure is entered, followed by a period and the name of the element declared within the structure.

12.2.15 The `switch` statement

Syntax:

```
switch(expression)
{
    case constant 1:
        statement 1;
        statement 2;
        ...
        break;
    case constant 2:
        statement 1;
        statement 2;
        ...
        break;
    ...

    default:
        ...
}
```

The value of the expression in `switch` is compared with the constants in the `case` expressions. When a match is found, the corresponding block of commands is executed.

It is wise to end a `case` block with `break`. The `default` statement, which we have already discussed, can be included in the `switch` construction if you choose. The commands following the `default` statement are carried out if none of the `case` conditions are fulfilled.

12.2.16 The `while` statement

Syntax:

```
while(expression)
    statement;
```

The statement (block) in the loop body is repeated as long as the `while` expression is true, that is, as long as the logical value of the expression is not zero. The expression can be replaced by a condition.

12.3 Variable types in C

The variable types can be divided into two parts: integral and floating-point variables. The variations of these two elementary types are as follows, although some C compilers do not support them all.

12.3.1 Integer variables

`char`	Single character value.
`int`	Integer value.
`short int`	Small integer value.
`long int`	Large integer value.
`unsigned int`	Positive integer, twice as large as regular `int`.
`unsigned short`	Positive `int`, twice as large as regular `short int`.
`unsigned long`	Positive `int`, twice as large as regular `long int`.

12.3.2 Floating-point variables

`float`	Floating-point number.
`double float`	Floating-point number with double precision.
`long float`	Treated like `double`.

12.4 Operators in C

C has a wealth of operators in comparison to BASIC. The following list includes the most important operators. The list is ordered according to execution priority, each level having lower priority than the last.

PRIORITY LEVEL 1

- ( )   Parentheses, function call
- [ ]   Array element
- ->   Structure pointer operator
- .   Structure variable operator

PRIORITY LEVEL 2

- -   Negative operator
- ++   Increment operator
- --   Decrement operator
- !   Logical negation operator
- *   Pointer operator
- &   Address operator

PRIORITY LEVEL 3

- *   Multiplication operator
- /   Division operator
- %   Modulo operator

PRIORITY LEVEL 4

- +   Addition operator
- -   Subtraction operator

PRIORITY LEVEL 5

- <<   Left-shift operator
- >>   Right-shift operator

PRIORITY LEVEL 6

- `<` Less than relation
- `<=` Less than or equal relation
- `>` Greater than relation
- `>=` Greater than or equal relation

PRIORITY LEVEL 7

- `==` Equality relation
- `!=` Inequality relation

PRIORITY LEVEL 8

- `&` Bitwise AND operator

PRIORITY LEVEL 9

- `^` Bitwise exclusive OR operator

PRIORITY LEVEL 10

- `|` Bitwise inclusive OR operator

PRIORITY LEVEL 11

- `&&` Logical AND operator

PRIORITY LEVEL 12

- `||` Logical OR operator

PRIORITY LEVEL 13

- `?:` Conditional assignment

Appendix A

Now that you worked through this book, what should you do next?

First it would be a good idea to strengthen your C programming skills, and the best way to do that is to get more practice. Write some new programs in C or convert some of your old BASIC programs into C. You should find the overview in the previous chapter helpful as you use the various C structures. If you want more precise information, you can find the appropriate sections of the book quickly with the index.

You have no doubt noticed that this book is just an introduction to C, although it is also a good reference work for programmers with experience in BASIC. Once you have strengthened your knowledge, you need more information about C. C is a relatively complex language and we didn't have enough room in this book to explain all of its features. The bibliography contains a number of books which will tell you more about C.

Appendix B:

More books on C

AT & T/Bell Laboratories, *C Programmer's Handbook*, Prentice-Hall, 1985.

Bean, *The Illustrated C Programming Book*, Prentice-Hall, 1985.

Birns, Brown, Muster, *UNIX for People*, Prentice-Hall, 1984.

Cooper, *Graphics Programming in C*, Sybex, 1985.

Costales, *C: From A to Z*, Prentice-Hall, 1985.

Hendrix, *The small C Handbook*, Prentice-Hall, 1985.

Harbison, Steele, *C: A Reference Manual*, Prentice-Hall, 1985.

Hogan, *The C Programmer's Handbook*, Brady, 1984.

Hunter, *Understanding C*, Sybex, 1985.

Joyce, *C by Example*, Addison-Wesley, 1985.

Kelley, *A Book on C*, Addison-Wesley, 1985.

Kernighan, Ritchie, *The C Programming Language*, Prentice-Hall, 1978.

Kochan, *Programming in C*, Hayden, 1983.

Moore, *Programming in C With a Bit of Unix*, Prentice-Hall, 1985.

Plum, *C Programming Guide Lines*, Prentice-Hall, 1984.

Plum, *Learning to Program in C*, Prentice-Hall, 1983.

Tondo, Gimpel, *The C Answer Book*, Prentice-Hall, 1985.

Traister, *Programming in C*, Prentice-Hall, 1985.

Traister, *Programming Halo Graphics in C*, Prentice-Hall, 1985.

Tyler, *Systems Programming in C*, Sybex, 1985.

Waite, Prata, Martin, *C Primer Plus*, Howard Sams, 1984.

Wotman, Sidebottom, *The C Programming Tutor*, Brady, 1984.

Zahn, *C Notes: A Guide to the C Programming Language*, Yourdon Press, 1979.

Index

`#define` 81-82, 198-199, 214
`&a` variables 27
`abort(0)` 133
address operator 28, 45, 71, 99, 101, 104, 173, 174, 196, 222
Alcyon C 5, 13, 25-27, 74-75
arithmetic operators 111-124
arrays 36-38, 43, 91-95, 99, 203, 206, 208
ASCII 24, 27, 61, 62, 74, 85, 86, 160
bit operators 123-124
`break` 211, 213
`case` 213
`char` 80, 203-205, 207, 212, 221
COBOL 3
comma 140-141
command extensions 75
comments 22-23, 42
comparison operators 116-119, 129-130
constants 81-83
`continue` 211, 214
control structures 31-34, 117, 127-158
conversion elements 52
data input 23, 38, 44, 49, 65, 67
data types 35, 79, 80, 83, 84, 91, 105, 193, 212
dBASE III 3
declaration headers 79
decrement operators 115-116, 144, 222
`default` 215
`define` 212, 214
DEF FN 197
Digital Research 4
`do` 215, 217, 221
`do-while` loop 148-149, 151-152
`double` 87, 212, 221
`else` 211, 216
`else if` 135-136, 216
End Of File(EOF) 24, 25, 38, 66, 75
equality operator 25, 29, 45, 130
`exit()` 131-133, 212

exponential notation 53
`extern` 211
`float` 87, 212, 221
`for` 17-19, 136-144, 147, 211, 216
FOR-NEXT 17-20, 137, 191
format instructions 15, 16, 52, 56
format specifiers 52, 53
functions 11, 41, 184-197
GEMDOS 10
`getchar()` 23-25, 37, 38, 44, 63, 65-68, 73-75, 86, 186
global variables 79, 90, 91, 93, 191
`goto` 154-157, 160, 211, 216, 217
header 79, 88, 195
hexadecimal 52
`if` 32-33, 128-130, 211, 213, 217, 222
`if-else` 32, 33, 45, 133-135
IF-THEN-ELSE 33
increment operator 31, 45, 115-116, 144, 222
indirection operator 58
inequality operator 25, 29, 45
infinite loop 137-140, 149, 150
input functions 65
integer constants 81, 82
integer data types 84
jump instructions 211
justification 54
keywords 211-212
Lattice 5
libraries 3, 183
local variables 90, 93-95, 196, 204
logical AND 45, 131, 223
loops 44, 138
macro 75, 198, 199, 214
`main()` 10-14
MC68000 4
Megamax compiler 5
Microsoft Corporation 145
mistakes 82, 165, 178
modulo operator 114, 222
NAND 121
negation operator 120, 121, 129, 222
nested `for` loops 141-144

nested while loops 148
new-line character 49, 177
null 217
octal 52
offset 104
operands 87
operators 31, 111, 112, 115-124, 129, 130, 172, 197, 222
outer interval limit 18
outputting numbers 54
Pascal 3, 11, 13, 203
pointer 26, 69, 70, 79, 95, 99-105, 107, 173, 174, 193, 195-197, 222
pointers and arrays 99-102
printf 12-18
putchar() 63, 65-68, 74, 75
puts() 27, 63, 65, 67, 68, 86, 118
record 203
return 218
Ritchie, Dennis 3, 154
scanf 68-72, 86, 131-134, 157, 159, 168, 171-174, 177, 179, 192-194, 196, 198, 212
scientific notation--see exponential notation
standard functions 25, 183
static 94, 95, 211
stdio.h 70, 74, 86, 118, 139, 186
string assignment 38
string variables 58-59, 82, 102
struct 203-208, 211-213, 215, 216, 218, 219, 222
SWAP 195-197
switch 3, 9, 80, 156-161, 211, 213, 215, 218, 219
symbolic constants. 35, 36, 80, 81, 90, 91, 198
text formatting 12-14, 56-57
unsigned 52, 83, 84, 87, 212, 221
value assignment 112-114, 146, 166, 169
variable type 88-90, 203
variables 14-15, 79-80, 203-206, 218, 221
while 211, 213, 215, 217, 220
while loop 20-22, 145-150, 211, 220

Optional Diskette

For your convenience, the 'C' program listings contained in this book are available on an SF354 formatted floppy disk. Due to diskette directory limitations the BASIC programs were not included. You should order the diskette if you want to use the programs, but don't want to type them in from the listings in the book.

All programs on the diskette have been fully tested. You can change the programs for your particular needs. The diskette is available for $14.95 plus $2.00 ($5.00 foreign) for postage and handling.

When ordering, please give your name and shipping address. Enclose a check, money order or credit card information. Mail your order to:

Abacus Software
5370 52nd. Street SE
Grand Rapids, MI 49508

Or for fast service, call **616/698-0330**.

ATARI® ST
REQUIRED READING

INTERNALS
Essential guide to learning the inside information of the ST. Detailed descriptions of sound & graphics chips, internal hardware, various ports, GEM. Commented BIOS listing. An indispensible reference for your library. 450pp. $19.95

GEM Programmer's Ref.
For serious programmers in need of detailed information on GEM. Written with an easy-to-understand format. All GEM examples are written in C and assembly. Required reading for the serious programmer. 450pp. $19.95

TRICKS & TIPS
Fantastic collection of programs and info for the ST. Complete programs include: super-fast RAM disk; timesaving printer spooler; color print hardcopy; plotter output hardcopy. Money saving tricks and tips. 200 pp. $19.95

GRAPHICS & SOUND
Detailed guide to understanding graphics & sound on the ST. 2D & 3D function plotters, Moiré patterns, various resolutions and graphic memory, fractals, waveform generation. Examples written in C, LOGO, BASIC and Modula2. $19.95

BASIC Training Guide
Indispensible handbook for beginning BASIC programmers. Learn fundamentals of programming. Flowcharting, numbering system, logical operators, program structures, bits & bytes, disk use, chapter quizzes. 200pp. $16.95

PRESENTING THE ST
Gives you an in-depth look at this sensational new computer. Discusses the architecture of the ST, working with GEM, the mouse, operating system, all the various interfaces, the 68000 chip and its instructions, LOGO. $16.95

MACHINE LANGUAGE
Program in the fastest language for your Atari ST. Learn the 68000 assembly language, its numbering system, use of registers, the structure & important details of the instruction set, and use of the internal system routines. 280pp $19.95

LOGO
Take control of your ATARI ST by learning LOGO—the easy-to-use, yet powerful language. Topics covered include structured programming, graphic movement, file handling and more. An excellent book for kids as well as adults. $19.95

PEEKS & POKES
Enhance your programs with the examples found within this book. Explores using the different languages BASIC, C, LOGO and machine language, using various interfaces, memory usage, reading and saving from and to disk, more. $16.95

BEGINNER'S GUIDE
Finally a book for those new to the ST wanting to understanding ST basics. Thoroughly understand your ST and its many devices. Learn the fundamentals of BASIC, LOGO and more. Complete with index, glossary and illustrations. +200pp $16.95

BASIC TO C
If you are already familiar with BASIC, learning C will be all that much easier. Shows the transition from a BASIC program, translated step by step, to the final C program. For all users interested in taking the next step. $19.95

The ATARI logo and ATARI ST are trademarks of Atari Corp.

Abacus  Software

5370 52nd Street SE Grand Rapids, MI 49508 Phone (616) 698-0330

Optional diskettes are available for all book titles at **$14.95**
Call **now** for the name of your nearest dealer. Or order directly from ABACUS with your MasterCard, VISA, or Amex card. Add $4.00 per order for postage and handling. Foreign add $10.00 per book. **Other software and books coming soon.** Call or write for your **free** catalog. Dealer inquiries welcome—over 1400 dealers nationwide.

We have the software you've been looking for!

DataTrieve
The electronic filing system for the ST

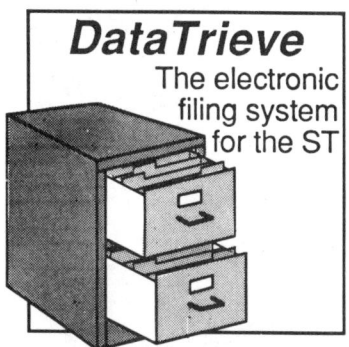

ST DataTrieve
Data management was never this easy. Online help screens; lightning-fast operation; tailorable display; user-definable edit masks; up to 64,000 records. Supports multiple files. Includes RAM-disk programs. Complete search, sort and file subsetting. Interfaces to TextPro. Easy yet powerful printer control. Includes five common database setups. **$49.95**

TextPro

Word processor for the ST

ST TextPro
Wordprocessor with professional features and easy-to-use! Full-screen editing with mouse or keyboard shortcuts. High speed input, scrolling and editing; sideways printing; multi-column output; flexible printer installation; automatic index and table of contents; up to 180 chars/line; 30 definable function keys; metafile output; much more. **$49.95**

PaintPro

For creative illustrations on the ST

ST PaintPro
Friendly, but powerful design and painting program. A *must* for everyone's artistic and graphics needs. Up to three windows. Cut & paste between windows. 36 user-defined fill patterns; definable line patterns; works in hi-med- & lo-res; accepts GDOS fonts. Double-sized picture format. **$49.95**
PaintPro Library #1 5 fonts, 300+ electronic, architectual, borders & clip art designs. **$19.95**

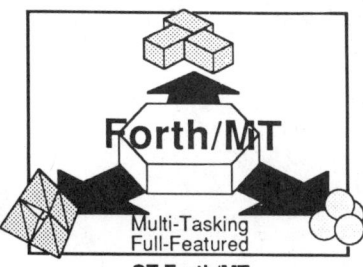

ST Forth/MT
Powerful, multi-tasking Forth for the ST. A complete, 32-bit implementation based on Forth-83 standard. Development aids: full screen editor, monitor, macro assembler. 1500+ word library. TOS/LINEA commands. Floating point and complex arithmetic. **$49.95**

AssemPro
The complete 68000 assembler development package for the ST

ST AssemPro
Professional developer's package includes editor, two-pass interactive assembler with error locator, online help including instruction address mode and GEM parameter information, monitor-debugger, disassembler and 68020 simulator, more. **$59.95**

PowerPlan ST
Full-powered Spreadsheet
37 math functions - 14 digit precision
Large size - over 4.2 billion cells
Multiple windows - up to 7
Graphics - 7 types of graphs

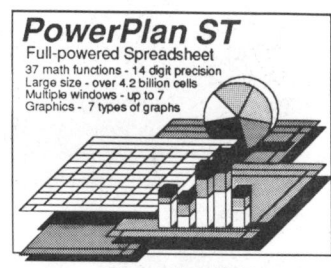

PowerPlan ST
Powerful analysis package. Large spreadsheet (65536 X 65536 cells), built-in calculator, notepad, and integrated graphics. 37 math functions, 14 digit-precision. Seven windows to show one of seven types of charts or another section of your spreadsheet. **$79.95**

ST and 1040ST are trademarks of Atari Corp.

Other software and books also available. Call or write for your **free catalog** or the name of your nearest dealer. Or order directly using your VISA, MC or Amex card. Add $4.00 per order for shipping and handling. Foreign orders add $10.00 per item. 30-day money back guarantee on software. Dealers inquires welcome—over 1500 dealers nationwide.

Abacus

Abacus Software • 5370 52nd Street SE
Grand Rapids, MI 49508 • Phone (616) 698-0330

Selected Abacus Products for the ATARI ST

DataRetrieve

(formerly FilePro ST)

Database management package for the Atari ST

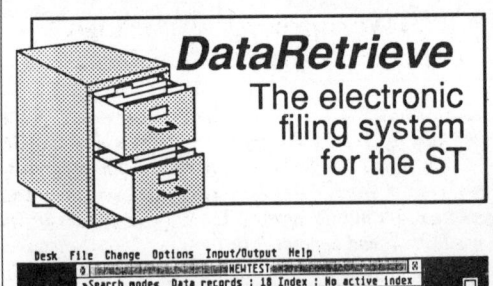

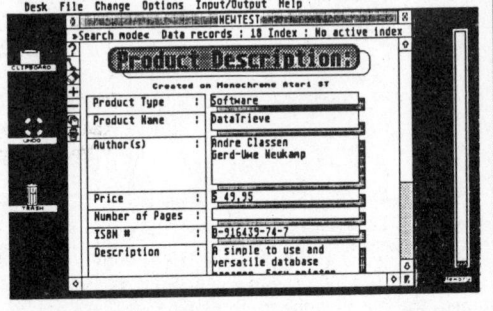

"DataRetrieve is the most versatile, and yet simple, data base manager available for the Atari 520ST/1040ST on the market to date."

—Bruce Mittleman
Atari Journal

DataRetrieve is one of Abacus' best-selling software packages for the Atari ST computers—it's received highest ratings from many leading computer magazines. **DataRetrieve** is perfect for your customers who need a powerful, yet easy to use database system at a moderate price of $49.95.

DataRetrieve's drop-down menus let the user quickly and easily define a file and enter information through screen templates. But even though it's easy to use, **DataRetrieve** is also powerful. **DataRetrieve** has fast search and sorting capabilities, a capacity of up to 64,000 records, and allows numeric values with up to 15 significant digits. **DataRetrieve** lets the user access data from up to four files simultaneously, indexes up to 20 different fields per file, supports multiple files, and has an integral editor for complete reporting capabilities.

DataRetrieve's screen templates are paintable for enhanced appearance on the screen and when printed, and data items may be displayed in multiple type styles and font sizes.

The package includes six predefined databases for mailing list, record/video albums, stamp and coin collection, recipes, home inventory and auto maintenance that users can customize to their own requirements. The templates may be printed on Rolodex cards, as well as 3 x 5 and 4 x 5 index cards. **DataRetrieve**'s built-in RAM disks support lightning-fast operation on the 1040ST. **DataRetrieve** interfaces to **TextPro** files, features easy printer control, many help screens, and a complete manual.

DataRetrieve works with Atari ST systems with one or more single- or double-sided disk drives. Works with either monochrome or color monitors. Printer optional.

DataRetrieve   Suggested Retail Price: **$49.95**

DataRetrieve Features:

- Easily define your files using drop-down menus
- Design screen mask size to 5000 by 5000 pixels
- Choose from six font sizes and six text styles
- Add circles, boxes and lines to screen masks
- Fast search and sort capabilities
- Handles records up to 64,000 characters in length
- Organize files with up to 20 indexes
- Access up to four files simultaneously
- Cut, past and copy data to other files
- Change file definitions and format
- Create subsets of files
- Interfaces with **TextPro** files
- Complete built-in reporting capabilities
- Change setup to support virtually any printer
- Add header, footer and page number to reports
- Define printer masks for all reporting needs
- Send output to screen, printer, disk or modem
- Includes and supports RAM disk for high-speed 1040ST operation
- Capacities: max. 2 billion characters per file
  max. 64,000 records per file
  max. 64,000 characters per record
  max. fields: limited only by record size
  max. 32,000 text characters per field
  max. 20 index fields per file
- Index precision: 3 to 20 characters
- Numeric precision: to 15 digits
- Numeric range $\pm 10^{-308}$ ti $\pm 10^{308}$

Atari ST, 520ST, 1040ST, TOS, ST BASIC and ST LOGO are trademarks or registered trademarks of Atari Corp.
GEM is a registered trademark of Digital Research Inc.

Selected Abacus Products for the

TextPro
Wordprocessing package for the Atari ST

"TextPro seems to be well thought out, easy, flexible anf fast. The program makes excellent use of the GEM interface and provides lots of small enhancements to make your work go more easily... if you have an ST and haven't moved up to a GEM word processor, pick up this one and become a text pro."

—John Kintz
ANTIC

"TextPro is the best wordprocessor available for the ST"
—Randy McSorley
Pacus Report

TextPro is a first-class word processor for the Atari ST that boasts dozens of features for the writer. It was designed by three writers to incorporate features that they wanted in a wordprocessor—the result is a superior package that suits the needs of all ST owners.

TextPro combines its "extra" features with easy operation, flexibility, and speed—but at a very reasonable price. The two-fingered typist will find **TextPro** to be a friendly, user-oriented program, with all the capabilities needed for fine writing and good-looking printouts. **Textpro** offers full-screen editing with mouse or keyboard shortcuts, as well as high-speed input, scrolling and editing. **TextPro** includes a number of easy to use formatting commands, fast and practical cursor positioning and multiple text styles.

Two of **TextPro**'s advanced features are automatic table of contents generation and index generation —capabilities usually found only on wordprocessing packages costing hundreds of dollars. **TextPro** can also print text horizontally (normal typewriter mode) or vertically (sideways). For that professional newsletter look, **TextPro** can print the text in columns—up to six columns per page in sideways mode.

The user can write form letters using the convenient Mail Merge option. **TextPro** also supports GEM-oriented fonts and type styles—text can be **bold**, underlined, *italic*, superscript, outlined, etc., and in a number of point sizes. **TextPro** even has advanced features for the programmer for development with its Non-document and C-sourcecode modes.

TextPro   Suggested Retail Price: **$49.95**

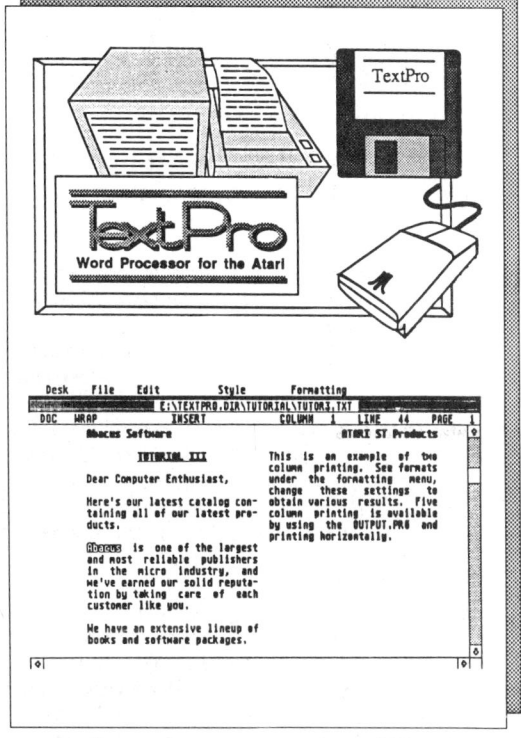

TextPro ST Features:

- Full screen editing with either mouse or keyboard
- Automatic index generation
- Automatic table of contents generation
- Up to 30 user-defined function keys, max. 160 characters per key
- Lines up to 180 characters using horizontal scrolling
- Automatic hyphenation
- Automatic wordwrap
- Variable number of tab stops
- Multiple-column output (maximum 5 columns)
- Sideways printing on Epson FX and compatibles
- Performs mail merge and document chaining
- Flexible and adaptable printer driver
- Supports RS-232 file transfer (computer-to-computer transfer possible)
- Detailed 65+ page manual

TextPro works with Atari ST systems with one or more single- or double-sided disk drives. Works with either monochrome or color ST monitors.

TexPro allows for flexible printer configurations with most popular dot-matrix printers.

Selected Abacus Products for the ATARI ST

PaintPro

Design and graphics software for the ST

PaintPro is a very friendly and very powerful package for drawing and design on the Atari ST computers that has many features other ST graphic programs don't have. Based on GEM™, **PaintPro** supports up to three active windows in all three resolutions—up to 640x400 or 640x800 (full page) on monochrome monitor, and 320 x 200 or 320 x 400 on a color monitor.

PaintPro's complete toolkit of functions includes text, fonts, brushes, spraypaint, pattern fills, boxes, circles and ellipses, copy, paste and zoom and others. Text can be typed in one of four directions—even upside down—and in one of six GEM fonts and eight sizes. **PaintPro** can even load pictures from "foreign" formats (ST LOGO, DEGAS, Neochrome and Doodle) for enhancement using **PaintPro**'s double-sized picture format. Hardcopy can be sent to most popular dot-matrix printers.

PaintPro Features :
- Works in all 3 resolutions (mono, low and medium)
- Four character modes (replace, transparent, inverse XOR)
- Four line thicknesses and user-definable line pattern
- Uses all standard ST fill patterns and user definable fill patterns
- Max. three windows (dependng on available memory)
- Resolution to 640 x400 or 640x800 pixels (mono version only)
- Up to six GDOS type fonts, in 8-, 9-, 10-, 14-, 16-, 18-, 24- and 36-point sizes
- Text can be printed in four directions
- Handles other GDOS compatible fonts, such as those in **PaintPro Library # 1**
- Blocks can be cut and pasted; mirrored horizontally and vertically; marked, saved in LOGO format, and recalled in LOGO
- Accepts **ST LOGO, DEGAS, Doodle & Neochrome** graphics
- Features help menus, full-screen display, and UNDO using the right mouse button
- Most dot-matrix printers can be easily adapted

PaintPro works with Atari ST systems with one or more single- or double-sided disk drives. Works with either monochrome or color ST monitors. Printer optional.

PaintPro   Suggested Retail Price: **$49.95**

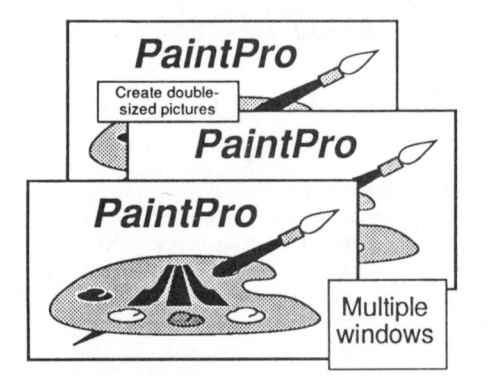
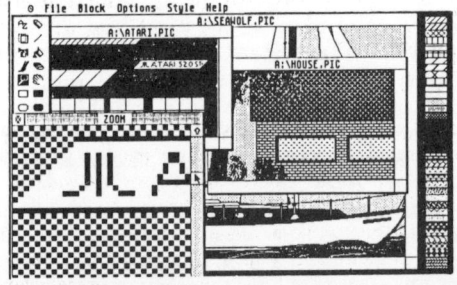
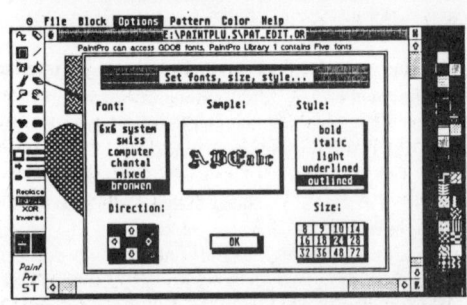
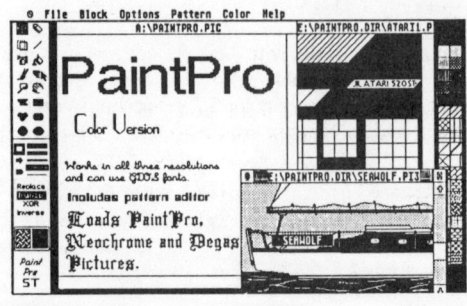

Selected Abacus Products for the ATARI ST

Chartpak ST

Professional-quality charts and graphs on the Atari ST

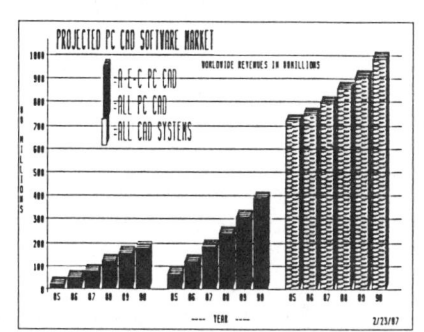

In the past few years, Roy Wainwright has earned a deserved reputation as a topnotch software author. **Chartpak ST** may well be his best work yet. **Chartpak ST** combines the features of his **Chartpak** programs for Commodore computers with the efficiency and power of GEM on the Atari ST.

Chartpak ST is a versatile package for the ST that lets the user make professional quality charts and graphs fast. Since it takes advantage of the ST's GEM functions, **Chartpak ST** combines speed and ease of use that was unimaginable til now.

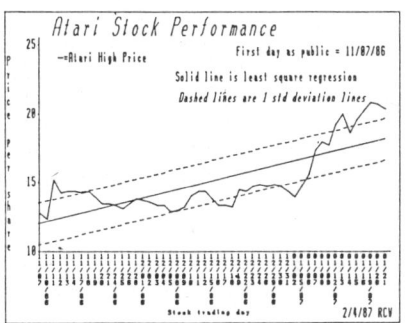

The user first inputs, saves and recalls his data using **Chartpak ST**'s menus, then defines the data positioning, scaling and labels. **Chartpak ST** also has routines for standard deviation, least squares and averaging if they are needed. Then, with a single command, your chart is drawn instantly in any of 8 different formats—and the user can change the format or resize it immediately to draw a different type of chart.

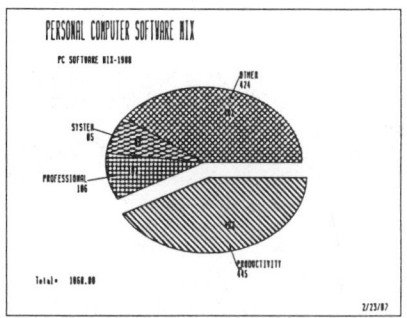

In addition to direct data input, **Chartpak ST** interfaces with ST spreadsheet programs spreadsheet programs (such as **PowerLedger ST**). Artwork can be imported from **PaintPro ST** or DEGAS. Hardcopy of the finshed graphic can be sent most dot-matrix printers. The results on both screen and paper are documents of truly professional quality.

Your customers will be amazed by the versatile, powerful graphing and charting capabilities of **Chartpak ST**.

Chartpak ST works with Atari ST systems with one or more single- or double-sided disk drives. Works with either monochrome or color ST monitors. Works with most popular dot-matrix printers (optional).

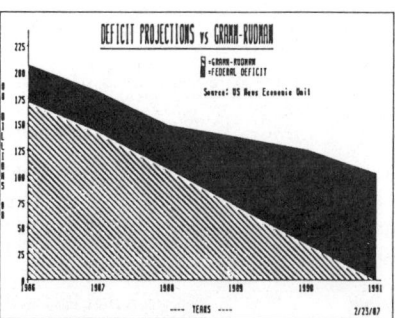

Chartpak ST   Suggested Retail Price: **$49.95**

Selected Abacus Products for the ATARI ST

AssemPro
Machine language development system for the Atari ST

"...I wish I had (AssemPro) a year and a half ago... it could have saved me hours and hours and hours."
—Kurt Madden
ST World

"The whole system is well designed and makes the rapid development of 68000 assembler programs very easy."
—Jeff Lewis
Input

AssemPro is a complete machine language development package for the Atari ST. It offers the user a single, comprehensive package for writing high speed ST programs in machine language, all at a very reasonable price.

AssemPro is completely GEM-based—this makes it easy to use. The powerful integrated editor is a breeze to use and even has helpful search, replace, block, upper/lower case conversion functions and user definable function keys. **AssemPro**'s extensive help menus summarizes hundreds of pages of reference material.

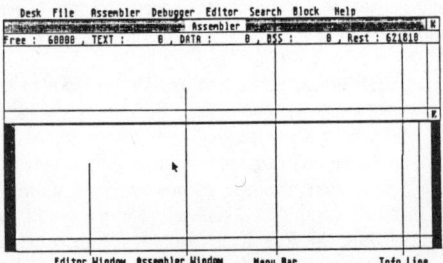

The fast macro assembler <u>assembles object code to either disk or memory.</u> If it finds an error, it lets you correct it (if possible) and continue. This feature alone can save the programmer countless hours of debugging.

The debugger is a pleasure to work with. It features single-step, breakpoint, disassembly, reassembly and 68020 emulation. It lets users thoroughly and conveniently test their programs immediately after assembly.

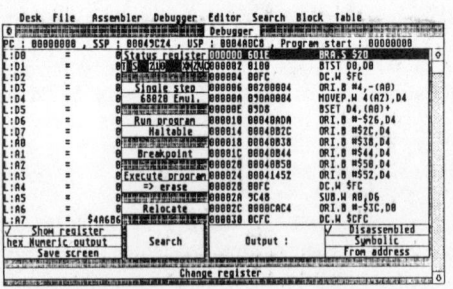

AssemPro Features:

- Full screen editor with dozens of powerful features
- Fast 68000 macro assembler assembles to disk or memory
- Powerful debugger with single-step, breakpoint, 68020 emulator, more
- Helpful tools such as disassembler and reassembler
- Includes comprehensive 175-page manual

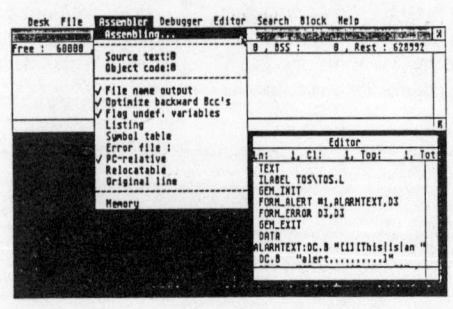

AssemPro Suggested retail price: **$59.95**

Atari ST, 520ST, 1040ST, TOS, ST BASIC and ST LOGO are trademarks or registered trademarks of Atari Corp.
GEM is a registered trademark of Digital Research Inc.